# the
# NEW
# HONOR
# CODE

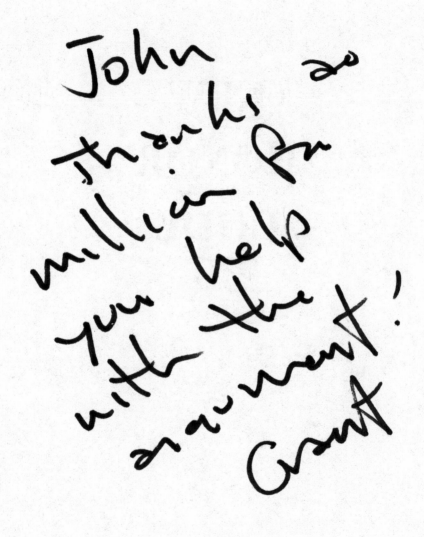

John

thanks a
million for
your help
with the
argument!

Grant

*the*

# NEW HONOR CODE

### A SIMPLE PLAN FOR RAISING OUR STANDARDS *and* RESTORING OUR GOOD NAMES

## GRANT McCRACKEN

*Tiller Press*

*New York   London   Toronto   Sydney   New Delhi*

TILLER PRESS

An Imprint of Simon & Schuster, Inc.
1230 Avenue of the Americas
New York, NY 10020

First Tiller Press hardcover edition December 2020

TILLER PRESS and colophon are trademarks of Simon & Schuster, Inc.

For information about special discounts for bulk purchases, please
contact Simon & Schuster Special Sales at 1-866-506-1949
or business@simonandschuster.com.

The Simon & Schuster Speakers Bureau can bring authors to your live event.
For more information or to book an event, contact the Simon & Schuster Speakers
Bureau at 1-866-248-3049 or visit our website at www.simonspeakers.com.

Interior design by Laura Levatino

Manufactured in the United States of America

1   3   5   7   9   10   8   6   4   2

Library of Congress Cataloging-in-Publication Data has been applied for.

ISBN 978-1-9821-5464-6
ISBN 978-1-9821-5466-0 (ebook)

*To Pamela, Zsa Zsa, Molly, and Vivienne*

# CONTENTS

*the*

# NEW

# HONOR

# CODE

# INTRODUCTION

Honor is fugitive. It's vagrant and miserable. It's on the lam. For hundreds of years and millions of people, it was a moral center of our lives. Now it's reduced to a cudgel we use to scold students who cheat on their exams. How sad. Honor used to govern so much more than undergraduates. Now it has to sleep in its car.

In America, we have the architecture of faith. We have an intensity of conviction. But it feels as if our moral compass is broken. Good people do bad things. And *bad* people—well, the bad people are just monstrous.

We need a return to honor.

I was compelled to write this book in order to restore honor to a place of honor. I seek to return it to the lives of Americans, even OxyContin producers, Lance Armstrong, Charlie Rose, Lori Loughlin, Larry Nassar, Jeffrey Epstein, and the millions of other Americans who can't manage to do the right thing.

1

The absence of honor is a terrible thing. We have men installing locks on their office doors, behind which they abuse their employees. We have men who put people on the company payroll purely to serve their sexual needs. These are not creatures who have merely slipped the bonds of morality. These are predators who believe they are *entitled* to prey on the vulnerable.

These men are wrecking machines, attacking, humiliating, and destroying the accomplishments of hardworking parents and teachers, to say nothing of the young woman who comes to a great job in the big city and thinks, *Wow, I made it.* In a single encounter, she is preyed upon. The executive is Grendel, that Anglo-Saxon beast from *Beowulf.* America is his mead hall.

But sexual predation is just the beginning. A bank called Wells Fargo decided recently it would issue credit cards to people who didn't want them. In the subprime debacle, an entire banking industry made loans that eventually destabilized first the housing market and then the economy. Politicians lie routinely. So do some religious officials. So do a lot of people charged with public responsibility and what we used to call "the public trust."

And when we're not lying, we're defaming. Speaking ill of the enemy, regardless of their actual crimes, is now standard on both sides of the aisle. Doubting their motives. Engaging in character assassination. We do not hesitate to say the most disreputable things about people who likely lead the same upstanding lives we do. We feast on these ruined reputations. We excoriate with glee.

And it's not just bad in the short term—it's bad business all around.

In the place of public trust, we are building a corrosive skepticism. We are ceasing to believe in our collective decency and driving ourselves into a wilderness from which we may not be able to escape.

I wanted to write this book for five reasons. The first was sheer shock at our scandalous state. Bad people doing terrible things. It just seemed endless. I thought, *Wow, if you think you can make a difference, you really should try.*

The second was a conversation I had with a state trooper I'll call Jim. This guy had invented his own honor code, or maybe he got it from the military. (You can decide when we talk about him in chapter 2.) Confronted by daily temptation, as we all are, he had found a way to resist it.

The third reason emerged when my wife and I got an email late in the day on a Sunday. Our neighbor Joan wanted to know if we would join her for what she called "latkes and screaming." She was inviting everyone in the immediate neighborhood to celebrate the last day of Hanukkah. She would supply the latkes, she said. Neighborhood kids were welcome to come and supply the screaming.

We sat, four of us, at a large round table surrounded by kids, ten of them, in constant motion and, yes, screaming. There were several fathers in the kitchen. There were several mothers in the living room. And the four of us at the table watching menorah candles burn down.

We talked about our respective religions. My wife is a Roman Catholic, a believer from childhood. David was raised a Protestant in northern Virginia. He fell away in early adulthood and then rebuilt his conviction through study and prayer. Joan is, at eighty-two, clear and beautifully learned in her Judaism. And then there's me, a guy raised in Canada as a middle-church Protestant. No longer religious, really (unless Canadian counts as a religion, sometimes I think it does). But I have vigorous opinions on what's right and what's wrong. Religious, no—moral, yes.

The conversation was tidal, rushing into the shore of what we could say, and back out into philosophical depths when things were less clear. It was careful. Philosophically careful. What could we say? What could we not? And respectful. *Oh, you think that! How interesting. No, we think this.*

It's common these days to give lip service to diversity, but here it was in the flesh. Deeply felt differences, passionately debated. With no fear of animosity. None.

This made for a mystery. How could ordinary people like us, so deeply committed to our public and private moralities, surrounded by many millions of equally religious and/or moral people, still find ourselves living in an America that feels corrupt and scandalous?

The fourth reason came when I was talking to a friend who's in charge of data for a large Silicon Valley company. Corporations can see American culture is changing. Michele (not her real name) said she was noticing data that could suggest a change in the way mothers thought about themselves and their kids. (If you ever want to get an anthropologist's attention, tell him child-rearing is changing. This is a chance to see what the future will look like in eighteen years.) You can't detect the future on the strength of something like this alone, so I started looking more broadly. (I run a device called the Griff that tracks and measures data and the changes these data reveal.)

When I checked, sure enough, the Griff was blinking, indicating that change was coming fast and furious. You could see a group of women beginning to ask whether they were raising their kids the best way. To learn more, I spoke to Lenore Skenazy, the author of *Free Range Kids: Giving Our Children the Freedom We Had Without Going Nuts with Worry.*[1] I took her to lunch and listened carefully.

And there was an Ancestry.com ad that caught my eye. Clearly, the people at Ancestry were hearing their clients talk in new ways. A character in the ad says that she sees her ancestors as survivors. What interests her, she says, are

> their lives, successes, hardships. That's part of what I want my
> kids to know. They come from people who were brave and
> took risks. Big risks.[2]

And I thought, *Hmm, if mothers are rethinking childhood, maybe it's time to bring honor back into the conversation.*

The fifth was forced upon me, as it was everyone else. The arrival of COVID-19, and the subsequent locking down of American culture, has been horrible. *The only silver lining*, I thought to myself, *is that maybe this is an opportunity for us to go back to square one and rebuild the moral compass.* COVID-19 has devastated our world in many ways. It would be wrong if we did not take advantage of the few opportunities it opens up. In the famous phrase of Stanford economist Paul Romer, a crisis is a terrible thing to waste.

*Okay*, I thought, *there is work to be done here*. For a very long time in the West, honor was a force inspiring good behavior and discouraging bad behavior. It had its problems—more about this in chapter 3—but as moral codes go, it punched above its weight.

I studied the history of honor as part of my PhD research, and it's recently occurred to me that maybe we could retrofit it for modern use. You could think of this book as an episode of *This Old House*, now called *This Old Idea*, "starring" me as Bob Vila as I try to show what we could do for honor with a little "home improvement."

In some ways, it's a preposterous idea. This honor code has no grand architecture. It doesn't depend on a specific church or philosophy. It doesn't aim to transform the spirit or the beast. Yet it may be just what we need right now—not a lofty moral goal, but a practical way to improve the chances that someone will do the right thing.

The new code of honor is not really about virtues, values, morals, or manners. It's a simple, clarifying set of inducements, meant to speak to the best in us and deter the worst.

I have tried to avoid a common error in books of this kind: to pretend no one has ever offered moral advice before. (*Here*, says the guru, *forget everything you have ever believed about ethics, and go with this, my new vision of life.*) On the contrary, one of the most useful aspects of honor, for our purposes, is that it recognizes we come from a diversity of experiences and life objectives. The advantage of this honor code is that it enables us to conduct ourselves well in spite of those differences.

My goal is to show why we struggle, as Americans especially, to make honor a part of daily life and culture. In researching honor, I spoke to cheesemongers, state troopers, and storytellers. The causes are complex, but these stories aren't—they're snapshots of our American past and present, lights toward the path back.

# CHAPTER 1

# *Symptoms of an Honor Shortage*

## 1.1 The Harvard Soccer Scandal

The Harvard soccer scandal of 2016 took people by surprise. The men's soccer team devised a so-called scouting report on the women's team, a spreadsheet in which each woman was assigned a sexual position and her desirability ranked. The report called one woman the "hottest and most STD ridden."[1]

Eventually this document found its way into the school newspaper, the *Harvard Crimson*, and all hell broke loose.

Drew Faust, president of the university, investigated and concluded that the "actions of the . . . team were not isolated to one year or the actions of a few individuals."[2] Oops.

Faust said that when she quizzed the members of the soccer team, they were "not initially forthcoming about their involvement." This is Ivy League code for "when confronted, they lied." Given an opportunity to do the right thing and confess their sins, these Harvard gentlemen choose to double down.

People hoped it might eventually serve as a teachable moment.

But alas, no. When Rakesh Khurana, the dean of the college, was asked repeatedly by the *Crimson* to comment on the first outbreak of the scandal, he replied,

> I was not Dean of Harvard College in 2012 and do not have knowledge of [the] particular email [in question], I cannot speak to the alleged conduct of these particular students.[3]

Alleged conduct? No knowledge? Was Khurana the dean or a lawyer? When presiding over a moral crisis as bad as anything Harvard had ever endured, he chose to duck.

But surely, people persisted, the team would come to its senses and apologize. And in fact, the 2016 team did send a letter of apology to the *Crimson*. But they also insisted that the letter run unsigned. The letter declares,

> We wholeheartedly promise to do anything in our power to build a more respectful and harmonious athletic field, class-room, and Harvard community.[4]

Anything, that is, but take responsibility. Stand up and be counted is what a decent person would do. The apology was a "crocodile confession"—all lamentation, no accountability.

What's even weirder is that the *Crimson accepted* the letter unsigned. Surely someone on staff protested, "An anonymous apology *isn't* an apology! That's *not* how apologies work." The letter ran anyway.

It was as if the scandal were designed to shine a light into every corner of the school. A group of students acted like scoundrels. When confronted, they lied. When asked to comment, Harvard administrators ducked. When given the chance to confess their sins, the players refused. When push came to shove, the *Crimson* caved. Everyone acted badly.

You might say, "Oh, for Pete's sake, this is just boys being boys. Lighten up a little. This is harmless fun."

It was not harmless fun.

Hannah Natanson was one of the women who played for Harvard. She quit the team in July of 2017. She told herself that the scouting report did not enter into her decision. But a few months later, she noticed something.

[T]he joy I used to find in exercise leached out. Every time I stepped outside in tight-fitting athletic clothes, I became hyper-conscious of my body. I curated a catalogue of faults: my ankles (spindly), my thighs (fleshy), my stomach (protruding), my shoulders (broad and manly).

I found myself constantly wondering whether passersby were watching me run.

I began to go on shorter runs. Then I began to run less often. One day midway through junior year, I stopped running entirely. I started avoiding mirrors. I stopped looking down in the shower. I went on sudden, absurd diets, vowing to alternate fasting with all-vegetable meals—before breaking all my own rules and ordering Falafel Corner to The Crimson at 2 or 3 or 4 a.m. I gained weight.

Like almost anyone my age, I logged onto Facebook a lot. I clicked through photos posted by members of the men's soccer team.

Some of them had graduated. They appeared to have moved to major cities. They had new jobs, girlfriends.

I remembered how, back in November 2016, some members of the women's team had wondered whether the scouting reports would affect the men's post-graduate lives. We asked each other, What will happen to them?

Nobody asked—aloud—what would happen to us.[5]

The scouting report was an act of violence.

The Twitter feed for the Harvard soccer team stopped abruptly on November 1, 2016, when the scandal hit. It started up again December 14 with a tweet pointing to an article on the official website of Harvard Athletics, Go Crimson. This article said, breathlessly and with no mention of the scandal, that the soccer team had given out awards for the 2016 season. In particular,

Senior Andrew Wheeler-Omiunu [was awarded the] Seamus Malin '62 Award . . . given to the player that best demonstrates sportsmanship, love of the game and commitment to the university.[6]

Really. Apparently, someone on the team that took a hammer to Hannah Natanson's self-esteem really believed in sportsmanship. Apparently, someone on the team that helped destroy Hannah's gift for the game really loved soccer. Apparently, someone on the team that had just brought disgrace and ridicule to Harvard was really committed to the university. Just saying. Go Crimson.[7]

———

The Harvard soccer scandal is many things. It is a failure of nerve, dignity, judgment, and decency. It was a failure to protect Harvard women from Harvard men. Everyone was diminished—female players, male players, the sport, the administrators, the dean, the *Crimson*, its journalists, the college, and the university. When given a chance to stand up and be counted, almost everybody folded.

The cynical among us might say, "Harvard has always been a place of deep and abiding hypocrisy. It was never about building character. In fact, it was a place the rich sent their children to learn how to conceal bad behavior behind good manners."

But this is an institution that has behaved honorably. Harvard sent nearly forty thousand students to fight in World Wars I and II. However, the soccer scandal didn't offer much evidence of that storied decency. Harvard is probably the oldest institution in America charged with improving the morals of American youth, and at some point, clearly, it faltered.

Could the scandal have been prevented by a new honor code at Harvard? What if there was a culture that moved one of the players to speak out? "Guys, this is stupid, diminishing, and wrong. This spreadsheet dishonors us because it dishonors them. It has to stop." In this

———

more perfect world, team members would come to their senses and say, "Oh, right. What were we thinking? Sorry."

The next question is the tough one: is it possible to build such a culture?

## 1.2 Wells Fargo and a Devil's Bargain

Richard Kovacevich blew his arm out while playing baseball at Stanford, ending his hopes for a career in the big leagues. So he got an MBA and went to work for General Mills selling consumer goods.

Then Kovacevich moved to Citicorp and eventually to Norwest Bank, where he had his big idea. *Why not sell banking the way we sell consumer goods?* he thought. Kovacevich began calling Norwest's banking services "products," its branches "stores," its bankers "salespeople," and its clients "customers."[8]

He also began encouraging his employees to cross-sell the products. Customers with one account were pressured to take out credit cards, mortgages, and loans, to make investments and buy insurance. "[Cross-selling] was his business model," says a former Norwest executive. "It was a religion. It very much was the culture."[9]

Kovacevich eventually became the CEO of Wells Fargo in 1998, where the practice took on new proportions. Wells Fargo was the nation's biggest retail bank at the time, with more than six thousand offices. Kovacevich prepared to turn this immense network into a selling machine, in what he called "the ultimate team sport." One of his colleagues called him "one of the most competitive people I have ever known."[10]

And this is where Kovacevich's experiment touched the life of Yesenia Guitron. Guitron was hired as a personal banker at Wells Fargo's St. Helena branch in California's Napa Valley in 2008. She was thrilled to get the job, and she read HR training documents with care, especially the Wells Fargo Code of Ethics and the Wells Fargo Team Member Handbook, in which the code was found.

By this time, Wells Fargo employees were deep into some dubious practices. They were opening online accounts for people who did not know how to use a computer. Most outrageously, they were opening accounts for people who did not actually exist.[11]

But even this doesn't begin to describe the full corruption of the organization Guitron had just joined. Wells Fargo was opening accounts for long-standing Wells Fargo customers without informing them. Naturally, customers did not pay fees on accounts they did not know they had. Naturally, collection agencies came calling. Naturally, credit ratings were downgraded. And the bank that wanted to loan its customers money was now actively damaging their ability to qualify. All in all, Wells Fargo was a weirdly lawless place.

In a Summer 2017 article in *Vanity Fair*, Bethany McLean itemizes still more dubious practices:

[E]mployees changed customers' phone numbers in the system so, if they complained, no one could get in touch with them. . . . But the worst, [Ivan Rodriguez, Wells Fargo employee] says, was the shredding. In order to get a signature on an account a customer didn't want, bankers would cut a signature out of an existing account, scan that through, and then shred the evidence.[12]

And then Wells Fargo told its people to shut up. "Management made it clear that no employee was allowed to complain about the unethical practices that were going on within the branch."

And customers were not the only victims. The cross-selling cult at Wells Fargo also punished its employees. One manager had district managers "run the gauntlet" dressed in ridiculous outfits. Another tells us that those who did not make their goals were "severely chastised and embarrassed in front of 60-plus managers . . . by the community banking president."[13]

The personal costs of this treatment were high. Wells Fargo bank manager Rita Murillo resigned in 2010, despite the fact that she did not have a job to go to and her husband was working part-time. The couple ended up losing their home. "'It all seemed worth the chance and the risk, rather than to deal with the mental abuse,' Murillo said. 'Just thinking about it gives me palpitations and a stomachache.'"[14]

Guitron suffered, too. "[E]verything was so tense at work, and it was miserable to go to work. Now, just thinking about it and talking about it is bringing back [the] headaches."[15] Many Wells Fargo employees endured the bank's behavior, but Guitron refused. Despite the fact that she was recently divorced and now the sole source of support for two kids, she complained to her supervisor, to the Ethics Hotline, to her bosses, and then to her bosses' bosses. "It's fraud, that's what it is," she said.[16]

But nothing happened. Well, one thing happened. Guitron got fired—for insubordination.[17]

It would be eight years before she got justice. In 2016, the Senate Banking Committee began to investigate. The *New York Times*, Reuters, and CBS gathered to cover the story and to interview Guitron, who, remarkably, managed to describe her experience with almost no trace of bitterness.

She won a public victory during the Senate Banking Committee meeting of September 20, 2016,[18] when Senator Jeff Merkley (D-Oregon) referred to her by name. He tore into the man who by this time was the CEO of Wells Fargo, John Stumpf. "This was a systemic problem that you benefited from enormously, the bank benefited from enormously, and you *are* scapegoating the people at the very bottom,"[19] Merkley said.

Within a month, Stumpf had been forced into retirement and relieved of $41 million of his compensation. Wells Fargo itself was fined a relatively paltry $185 million. It fired 5,300 employees.[20] Senator Tim Scott (R-South Carolina) called Wells Fargo a "toxic culture." *American Banker* said Wells Fargo had a "propensity to bathe its brand in scandal."[21]

In the end, the little guy won—sort of. Guitron was vindicated.

Wells Fargo suffered reputational damage from which it will never fully recover. The Senate moved on to other things. The journalists packed up and went away. The world returned to business as usual.

But something is missing. Isn't it? It's still not clear whether Wells Fargo or its senior managers ever really acknowledged the disgrace they had brought upon themselves—or the pain they caused others. In that Senate Banking Committee meeting, Stumpf presented himself as a mild-mannered man eager to reassure the committee that the only thing he really cared about was fixing Wells Fargo. Not a charm offensive, exactly; more like milquetoast theater. He was agreeable to the point of obsequiousness, as if he believed an oil slick of deference would make the crisis go away. He blinked throughout Merkley's attack, like a gentle boy being tormented by a schoolyard bully.

As you watch Stumpf, you might even find yourself lulled into a forgiving mood. Maybe Wells Fargo is not so bad after all! Maybe it was just a couple of bad apples! Maybe no one really knew! And that's when, hopefully, you feel a searing pain in your cerebellum and think, *Wait a second! Wells Fargo invented accounts for phantom clients and eleven-year-old children, all the while falsifying records to avoid detection and redress. This bank destroyed credit ratings, humiliated employees, and retaliated against those who dared criticize them. Wells Fargo was the West Coast bank without a moral compass. It was a monster by the sea, something that had crawled up out of the Pacific to feast on trusting Americans.*

And at this point, we want a different Stumpf. We want him to express regret, remorse, and humiliation before the Senate Banking Committee. We want him to drop the servility and give us some indication he grasps that his bank's behavior was lawless, abusive, and criminal—and that he, as the man at the top, is responsible. That's key. You. Stumpf. Responsible.

But it can't merely be a matter of theater. We need to create a culture in which the people in charge are personally and professionally diminished by the scandal. But in our current reality, an executive like him is tempted by a devil's bargain. If he can just ignore immoral behavior, behold the riches that come: millions in salary, millions more in stock options, beautiful homes, private clubs, business jets, personal chefs, a life of absolute security, every little whim indulged.

Let's replace the devil's bargain with an angel's threat. Forgive (or ignore) the corruption in your company and you can no longer look at yourself in the mirror. You can no longer live with yourself. You have destroyed your personal sense of dignity. You will now scorn yourself the way you scorn others. In the angel's threat, self-respect matters just as much—sometimes more—than the respect of others.

Ideally, we would build a culture that threatens the CEO with the loss of his self-respect *and* his social respect. The first moment the CEO detects the scent of scandal, he would say, "Hold everything. The reputation of my bank is in jeopardy. More important, *my* reputation hangs in the balance. And you don't pay me enough to compromise my self-respect. Whatever this is, it has to stop."

Create a culture like this and honor rushes in.

## 1.3 The Case of Charlie Rose

Charlie Rose used to be my hero. He started his eponymous PBS interview show in 1991, while Johnny Carson was still on the air. Occasionally, on *The Tonight Show*, a guest would say something a little bit obscure, and Johnny would look to the camera and say, "I did not know that." This was greeted by rapturous applause from the late-night audience, as if *not knowing* was witty or winning. Charlie Rose found a way to smuggle ideas into this world.[22]

But there was nothing heroic about the man Sophie Gayter, a former staffer at *60 Minutes*, encountered. Ms. Gayter says Charlie Rose groped her buttocks as they walked down an office hallway. She remembers,

> People said what they wanted to you, people did what they wanted to you.[23]

It's a haunting line. So bleak, so fatalistic, so Soviet. And so head-hurtingly ironic. A man of ideas stalking young women in Manhattan hallways.[24]

We know what was *supposed* to happen. Inevitably, a TV show brings together seasoned producers (mostly men) and youthful journalists (often women). Generally speaking, the playbook was clear. The producers were supposed to *lead*, offering instruction, support, and professional courtesy. They did not stand in loco parentis (in place of parent). That moment had passed. But they were supposed to guide and educate. Their role was not parental but maybe a little avuncular (uncle-ish). Over and above this standard managerial package, the producer, at his or her discretion, might add a "We're rooting for you, kid" solicitude. And that's it. This is as far as the producer could go.

Call it the "roles and rules" model. The producers had a *role*. And at any given moment, a producer could consult this role to determine the *rules* of conduct. What role have I been assigned in my relationship to this young woman? That of producer. Check. What rules govern what a producer owes to a journalist? Guidance and advice. Check and check. And if I want to involve myself a little more deeply in this career, what more can I do? Offer career guidance in the form of navigational advice and moral support. Check, check, and check.

Groping a woman's buttocks? This was an obvious violation of the role and rules with which Charlie Rose was charged. Simple, really. Pretty obvious, actually. And apparently a complete mystery to Charlie Rose.

There's no question the "roles and rules" approach to morality is imperfect. Many people fail to live up to it. Many, no doubt, use it as protective cover for bad behavior. But in its purest form, it gives clarity. You know what to do.

These days, people seem to have no clue what to do. It's as if every relationship, even professionally, starts from zero, with both sides asking, "Okay, how are we going to play this?"

How disgracefully dumb. This is what *culture* is for. It codifies roles and rules. It captures good and decent practice, and passes it along from one generation to the next, precisely so that every human two-some *doesn't* have to start from zero.

What the hell happened? How did we drift this far out of our shipping lanes? What happened to honor? Stay tuned to find out.

## 1.4 Lance Armstrong: The Nerve of This Guy

Consider this reflection on the career and reputation of Lance Armstrong, by the British journalist Barry Glendenning:

> In an interview with the BBC in 2015, Armstrong described his behaviour over 15 years, particularly his treatment of "a dozen or so people" whose characters, reputations and careers he attempted to destroy in a bid to save his own as "totally regrettable and completely inexcusable." Adding that he had apologies accepted by a few of those from whom he sought forgiveness, he conceded he couldn't keep apologising forever: "We all want to be forgiven. There's a lot of really, really bad people that want to be forgiven that will never be forgiven and I might be somewhat in that camp."[25]

Armstrong admits that his behavior was "completely inexcusable." When you corrupt a sport, when you steal honors from athletes who don't cheat, and when you seek to destroy those who object to your behavior, you are engaged in behavior that *is* completely inexcusable. So high marks there, Mr. Armstrong.

Armstrong also admits there are "really, really bad people," that he "might be somewhat in that camp," and that this might make him someone who "will never be forgiven."

Right again. There appears to be a flicker of self-knowledge here, which is, pathetically, more than we can say for some of his compatriots in this book. Lance Armstrong has at least glimpsed who and what he is.

But self-knowledge is only as good as what you do with it. Mr. Armstrong is now several years into a campaign to renew his respectability. Evidently, he does not care that he is "somewhat in the camp" of "really, really bad people." Armstrong believes he deserves our attention, that he is entitled to comment on the sport he helped corrupt, that he ought to have his credibility as a public figure restored, that he should be an inspiration to other athletes and even kids. So, incorrigible and beyond hope after all.

Yet the campaign appears to be working. Armstrong told CNBC in 2018 that he expected his podcast to bring in between $700,000 and $1 million over the course of his three-week coverage of the Tour de France. Endorsements are beginning once more to flow. Some people are prepared to defend him in public, to plead this case.[26] Everyone in cycling dopes, the argument goes; Armstrong was just the one who got caught. And let's just forget about those "people whose characters, reputations and careers [Armstrong] attempted to destroy in a bid to save his own."

In a sense, his campaign should not surprise us. What could be more natural, coming from someone who has always expected to lie, cheat, and bully with impunity? On the other hand, perhaps it *should* astonish us that people are beginning to forgive the guy. What is wrong with us?

———

Which brings us to honor.

When Lance Armstrong was deciding to dope or not, I think we can speculate he was making a simple calculation. It *might* have gone something like this.

> *Doping will help me win. Yes, I might get caught, but I can survive the costs of discovery. I will not lose everything. In the worst case, I will endure a period of disgrace. But I will get a shot at rehabilitation and a chance to repair my reputation. Talk shows will open to me. Endorsements will return. I'll be back in business.*[27]

This is not what happens in a world constrained by honor. The cost is clear and irrevocable. Do something "completely inexcusable" and you will not be excused. No one will listen to your podcast. No one will want you as an endorser. You are done. You will not be allowed back into public life.

This makes for a very different calculation. The would-be cheater contemplates the ways he can cheat to get an edge in his sport. In our society, this is a risk–benefit calculation. There is no real fear of banishment. In this calculation, it is pretty much all benefit. But in a society based on honor, we have something to lose. And it's not just our popularity, our currency, or our celebrity. It's our self-worth. And unlike popularity, currency, or celebrity, this is very hard to get back.

## 1.5 Stuffed-Shirt Honor

Years ago, I worked at a museum. My colleagues were arts administrators, academics, and civil servants. There seemed to be a lot of award ceremonies of one kind or another. In fact, it felt like we spent much of our time conspiring to give awards to other people, chiefly, I began to think, because we hoped to get awards in return. There was a lot of honoring going on.

It was very tedious. On one occasion, I went to a reception on a Monday. It wasn't until the next day that I discovered my error. The event I had intended to go to was, in fact, on Tuesday. Yet it hardly mattered. I met all the same people, talked about all the same things, added my voice to the same chorus of self-congratulation. The world of the arts didn't even care which event I went to. They were pretty much interchangeable.

If you asked people what they thought they were doing at these events, I'm pretty sure they would have told you they were "honoring" the arts. The recipients have done good works of some kind or other. In reward, they are *honored*.

Eventually, I came to think of it as the "stuffed-shirt" model of honor. Or the "I-own-a-tuxedo" model of honor. After all, it makes sense to invest in a tuxedo when the return might be an award of your own.

But does it really matter if fat cats sit around giving one another honors? I mean, nobody gets hurt, right?

Wrong.

For one thing, it empowers the pointlessly powerful. An award, well, that's just ducky. Now everyone has to treat them with new respect. A little respect is a dangerous thing. It can make a small-minded person smaller-minded still—or intolerable, in some cases.

But more important, the process brings discredit on the very idea of honor. It suggests that honor is the province of the social and professional elites, whom others already dislike and distrust. It reduces honor to tuxedo status: it doesn't actually signify anything. It's really just a way of showing off.

When true honor is replaced by self-congratulation, it's just another pretext for the already advantaged to make deals and cement their insider advantage. If you don't have a place at that table, there are things you'll miss out on, schools your kids won't be going to. This is an honor system that rewards all the wrong people for all the wrong reasons.

Surely, it's time to see that it is wrong to merely honor the timeservers, the people who go along to get along, the ones who play their cards just right in order to get that promotion, full professorship, order of merit. To give honor to the timeservers and the stuffed shirts is not only to fail fundamentally to see the *purpose* of honor; it degrades the very idea. It takes a glorious aristocratic idea and turns it into a hollow shell.

# CHAPTER 2

# Unsung Heroes

So who are the people we should be honoring instead? I had a look around my community, and it didn't take long to find some unsung heroes.

## 2.1 Making More Bobs

Imagine you are eighty years old and living on $10,000 a year. Chances are you're going to end up in a rooming house, in a small room. You will have a dorm-size fridge and a hot plate. You may or may not have a washroom of your own. There may or may not be elevators and ramps. Your hip goes out? Why, that's too bad. It takes you twenty minutes to climb those stairs? Well, you've got plenty of time, don't you? You're not sure about some of the people you're living with. You lock your door, and you wish that was enough to keep out the noises and smells. You are not allowed a dog or a cat for company. There are lots of people in your rooming house, but no one looks like friend material.

This is where Bob comes in. Bob volunteers for Hill Top Homes, an affordable housing community in Norwalk, Connecticut, designed for seniors and the mobility impaired, and subsidized by the US Department of Housing and Urban Development (HUD). As of the year 2006, HUD residents have a (national) average age of seventy-nine and annual income of $10,018. Hill Top Homes gives people independence and, if needed, help with things like dressing, bathing, housekeeping, and transportation. Bob got involved when Hill Top Homes was turning forty years old and beginning to deteriorate; he helped secure another round of HUD funding. (And yes, you can have a dog or a cat at Hill Top Homes.) Bob is saving seniors from the indignities of rooming houses—and he's doing it without compensation.

That's just for starters. Bob also serves the Rowayton United Methodist Church, the Stamford Hospital Foundation, the Roton Point Association, the Rowayton Civic Association, the Boy Scouts of Fairfield County, the Sixth Taxing District (Rowayton), Meals on Wheels of Stamford and Darien, and Fairfield County's Community Foundation.

In short, Bob is a Frank Capra kind of guy. Capra's beloved movie *It's a Wonderful Life* examines the difference a person can make to his community. Recall the scene in which the angel Clarence Odbody (Henry Travers) takes George Bailey (Jimmy Stewart) around Bedford Falls, now Pottersville, to show him what the place would look like without his influence. If we reran the history of our town without Bob Eydt, it would be a different place. Not as desperate as

Pottersville, but certainly smaller and meaner. In Rousseau's language, it would be more *aggregation* and less *association*.[1]

And while we're quoting prototypical French anthropologists, Bob also put me in mind of Alexis de Tocqueville, the political theorist who visited America in the middle nineteenth century and noticed that Americans had a peculiar genius for volunteer associations.[2] Bob has a steadfast belief in the ability of an association to do good work, even when it means dealing with people who would rather blow up a meeting than get stuff done.

———

I wouldn't know any of this if Bob weren't my neighbor. We sometimes walk together with his dog Grey. I started to ask him what he knows about our little town (anthropologists pry for a living), and as the details rolled out, I couldn't believe the extent of his sacrifice and commitment—and he never would have told me of his own accord.

So what's really in it for Bob? How do we reward him for his extraordinary service to this town? It turns out (yes, I asked about this, too) Bob is not really rewarded at all. When you ask him, he says, "I'm just trying to give back." Not only does Bob not get paid, he doesn't even get much in the way of acknowledgment or admiration. Most people don't know how active he is.

Clearly, we need more Bobs. That's the endgame of this book. An effective honor code is designed to make more Bobs.

## 2.2 State Trooper Jim

A couple of years ago, I was engaged by the Ford Foundation to do a study of American culture. What, the foundation wanted to know, had happened to the *middle* of American politics?

Americans used to cluster in the middle. They prided themselves on their ability to see both sides. To hew to the middle was for millions a point of pride.

Sometime around 2008, Americans began moving left and right.[3] The middle was being hollowed out. Conversations began to break down. One person would say to another, "You just don't get it." And when people start talking like this, an anthropologist's blood runs cold. People are disagreeing not on points of policy but basic assumptions. The common ground of American politics, once relatively solid, was now melting into air.

"Go look," my handlers said. "Find out what happened."

A lot had happened. I talked to people still reeling from the sub-prime mortgage debacle. They had lost incomes, homes, and neighborhoods. I talked to good old boys who believed themselves to be the victims of the effort to end prejudice. I talked to actual victims of prejudice. I talked to embattled mothers trying to sustain their families with self-help therapies and pyramid-marketing schemes. I talked to mothers trying to sustain their families on government subsidies and support programs. People were scrambling. They were angry and desperate. You could see Trump coming. Not the man himself—this was 2013, after all. But the waves of resentment that would carry an outsider to office were already visible and building.[4]

I met one guy, let's call him Jim.[5] Jim was a middle-aged husband and father. He had been a state trooper for twenty years, and he could feel the perturbations running through American culture, but he wasn't feeling much confusion personally. Jim was well. Jim was clear.

Anthropology is a charm offensive, or it tries to be. You persuade someone to let you into their home. Coffee is offered. Pets are penned up. Compliments are exchanged. Small talk goes back and forth. You always take that cup of coffee. You always express delight upon meeting the family's cherished cat or dog. This is not mere ceremony. You are signaling that you are someone who grasps that he's here on sufferance. It is, after all, all about *them*. That has to be clear.

The trick is to get past the awkwardness that exists between perfect strangers and, in the course of the next hour or two, get to a frank exchange of views.

We make the most of the journey. We do the long climb out of the foothills of false starts and long pauses through the uplands of growing acquaintance until we break out of the last of the alpine pines into a clearing. Usually, this gives you a vista. From here some part of American life comes into view.

Unfortunately, Jim isn't going for it.

It isn't that he's standoffish. It's not that he needs coaxing. I have done a lot of interviews, and usually I can tell why a wheel has come off, and, with a little effort, get it back on. But I can't tell what happened with Jim. Something in his facial expression and body posture says, "I don't need you. I don't need this." He isn't being aggressive, rude, or hostile. He's just not going to budge.

Then he starts telling me about what it's like to be a state trooper. He's always pulling people over on the highway. He walks up to the driver's side of the car. The window rolls down. And there is something about the way some people look at him, Jim says, and he can see it coming.

Several times a week, the driver tries to buy his or her way out of a ticket. "They begin with money. If they're really desperate, they go to drugs. And if they are really, really desperate, they go to sex. It happens more often than you would think."

Now I can see what I'm looking at. Jim found a way to resist temptation. He built a wall. Over the course of twenty years, he's been tempted thousands of times. He's had to say no thousands of times. He's been standing on a slippery slope, and he's kept his footing.

In a culture that's always blurring the lines between what's okay and what is not, Jim is clear. He built his own moral compass. He lives a life of clarity. And that's what's sitting across the table from me. It's not pride. It's self-possession.

I press Jim. "I mean, how do you do it?" Jim looks at me with pity. *If you have to ask*, he seems to say, *you will never see*. What he sees across the table is a softhearted anthropologist. Nice enough. But disciplined? Probably not. (Am too.)

I'm reeling. Ethnography is empathy. You listen until you go, "Oh, like that," and you suddenly see the world as they do. I'm trying that now. Something flickers in my head. An idea that I haven't thought about for thirty years.

———

Honor. I'm looking at honor.

How many times are the rest of us tempted? How walled are we? Or is it just a matter of time before the world finds the temptation we can't resist? And it *will* keep trying. And with Jim, it tries several times a week. The world has been throwing this temptation at Jim for a couple of decades. And he found a way to stand firm.

I can't believe my eyes. My head is firing in all directions. Somewhere way at the back, someone is shouting, "Are you kidding me?" Then there's the shouting on the outside. It's me, breaking with protocol, yelling at Jim, "You're the last honorable man!"

I regret this immediately (and report it here with embarrassment). But even allowing for my chronic condition (late-onset hyperbole), this feels like a finding.

Jim narrows his eyes and looks at me.

"Last honorable man?"

He's not going *there*.

It feels like Jims are exceedingly hard to find. Lying, stealing, influence peddling, abuse, self serving, these are all commonplace. But not here upstate. Jim's home is Shangri-La, a hideout for honor.

Jim's self-possession has rules. Do not surrender control to others. Do not care what they think of you. Do not seek their approval. Do not depend on things external to yourself, be it money, drugs, or sex. Temptation will come in many forms. (It could even be an anthropologist shouting outlandish praise at you in your living room.) Refuse this, too. The moment you accept someone's praise, you no longer belong fully to yourself.

This is Jim's method. It's not the only way to achieve honor, but it works for him. Jim has a boundary, an armor, a clarity. He's got a "me" that separates him from temptation on the highway. He has a discipline that says, "That's that. I'm this."

Does Jim have honor? Yes, he does. He is the master of his domain. But is Jim *honored*? The answer here is not so clear. Certainly some people would give Jim credit for his high moral standing, his absolute self-discipline. His family and neighbors no doubt see and respect these qualities. But does our larger society honor him?

When I was first thinking about writing this book, I approached various agents and publishers to see who might be interested. And at first there was excitement in some quarters. This cooled quickly when people got a look at the outline for the book. One person in particular was offended by the idea that I should want to treat a state trooper as an exemplar of honor. For this New York liberal, there wasn't anything noble about a state trooper. In fact, there was something a little iffy about writing a book about honor, and this just proved it. It was as if I was being told to exalt the right people—not, you know, thugs on motorcycles.

So, no, Jim doesn't get the honor he deserves. This is a problem we have to fix.

## 2.3 Community Organizer Erin

It took a while for me to register that the Potting Shed isn't a potting shed. It's run by Erin Combs, Samira Schmitz, and Tory Woodruff as a part of a larger group, the Rowayton Gardeners. Traditionally, the Gardeners tended flower plots on traffic islands and brought color to nooks and crannies around town. They made wreaths for the holidays. They beautified the town. But the Potting Shed crew, and especially Erin, had other ideas.

When Erin moved to Connecticut from Brooklyn in 2008, she wasn't sure what to expect. Was she going to have to play a lot of tennis? Wear more skirts? She thought she might get involved with the gardening club, but her early proposals proved controversial. "Versailles!" people said. "You want to turn our town into Versailles!"

Erin's ideas were a lot like Erin—exuberant and enterprising. And to people accustomed to the rhythms of a small town, they felt a little bit like a land grab. What was she up to? What was she after? But as I sat listening to her in her home one winter's day, I thought, *"Land grab" is not the thing to fear from this woman*. The Potting Shed was clearly up to something altogether more seditious.

Erin gives off generosity. It's not a saintly generosity, the kind that comes from people who answer to a higher calling. No, it's the kind that comes from people who are constitutionally incapable of seeing the world in a zero-sum way. It's obvious to Erin that when you win, she wins, and vice versa. The only null spot for people like Erin is inactivity. We both lose when we do nothing, she reasons, so let's do something. Anything, if at least modestly intelligent and well executed, is good for our little town on the sound.

This is what leadership often looks like, but I can see how it might provoke anxiety. Who is this newly arrived bundle of initiative, and what if she turns our town upside down? Eventually, the town began to see that Erin was, as she puts it, not planning to build a Versailles— "or even a Starbucks," she says wryly—and they let her into the garden group. And before long, of course, she was running it. To keep the risk small, she asked for the potting shed.

Once a storage space, the Potting Shed is now more like a community center. It's a place where stuff happens. Erin, Samira, and Tory see it as a place for kids to play. Like most Americans, Rowaytonites keep their kids on a short leash. For some this amounts to virtual house arrest. Kids are not allowed out. They are constantly observed and managed and controlled. This makes the Potting Shed one of their favorite places. Before long they are turning cartwheels, brandishing sunflower stalks, and baying for the heads of their "enemies." It's absolute pandemonium. These kids are making up for lost play.

Erin is accustomed to parents coming up to her and saying, "I'm so glad you do this"—in a tone that suggests they are anything but glad. The implication is, "This is really nuts and there's a good chance that you are, too." It's an ambivalence. These parents can see how much "sunflower combat" means to their kids, but they still find the whole thing a little bit, well, scary. Erin could mention that Rowayton was a second home for Maurice Sendak when he was writing *Where the Wild Things Are*. But she doesn't. That would be zero-sum.

Lots of things now happen at the Potting Shed. There are evenings when people are invited to build fairy houses. This means grabbing a glue gun and putting together a little place about five inches high. Dads, especially, rise to the occasion for some reason. There are no rules for fairy houses. (I was shocked to learn there's no building code at all.)

The Potting Shed also stages pumpkin carving. Americans used to have a formula for this Halloween activity: three triangles and a crenellated tooth or two. The Potting Shed has a bigger design envelope. Power tools are required. Imagination is unleashed. Triangles give way to fluid, menacing lines. Before you know it, something wicked this way comes to pumpkins.

There's also a film series. Films like *Grey Gardens* are projected on a bedsheet for an audience on lawn chairs, the slippery reality inside the film threatening to make a slippery reality outside the film. Delicious. Scary. Certainly not Versailles. No, something much worse.

The old gardening club beautified, because that's what gardens were for, traditionally—making a good impression. Putting your best face forward. And doing this is, as Erving Goffman told us, something more than putting on an exterior show. It's designed to signal that we're good, decent, proud, reliable, and self-respecting. These are ancient values and they have driven the behavior of the middle class ever since they took over duties from Lady Bountiful, that creature who deigned to make everyone's world better by aesthetic improvement and her own noble example. The old garden club had a civilizing mission.

It's a little corny to say so, but Erin's is something more like an "uncivilizing mission." She wants to see what happens when we set aside fatuous manners and stop worrying about impressions. When we give up the insincerities of social life and escape culture's conventions—especially for the sake of kids desperate to escape house arrest.

This is a good and noble mission, but there is little honor in it for Erin. In fact, Erin avoids getting credit for what she does. After our interview, I wrote up these notes and sent them to her, but I never heard back. So when I saw her at the grocery store, I stopped her. She was anxious.

"Oh, I'm not sure I like the attention. I mean, this is a little embarrassing. I don't want people thinking I am taking all the credit. That's the last time they will work with me, believe me."

Erin is doing something remarkable for this little town. If anyone deserves credit and honor it's her. But not only is she not getting honor, she is working hard to make sure she never does. There's something dangerous about honor in my little town. The more honor she gets, Erin thinks, the less good she can create. Talk about perverse incentives! It's time to turn that equation around.

## 2.4 Cheesemonger Ken

Happily, there are others in my community who are decidedly not unsung. In fact, they are frankly and publicly adored. And I found myself wondering, what makes these people different?

Let's start with Ken. He owns Darien Cheese and Fine Foods, a much-loved local store.

Here's a quote from Stacey Bewkes's blog, Quintessence:

In my food universe, Ken Skovron IS the big cheese. As the owner of Darien Cheese, Ken is one of the most well-respected specialty food shop owners around. I've been buying delectable products at this fabulous store for over 20 years.

Most of Ken's products still come from Europe, where it all started. And within this culture, he searches out the truly authentic and unique. This is what's closest to his heart and the raison d'être of his business—introducing customers to these special handmade products and their heritage. . . .

Shopping at Darien Cheese is an intimate experience—Ken and his staff take the time to find out exactly what you want, even if you don't know yourself. You are never rushed, even during the holidays when the double line extends well out onto the sidewalk. You are always encouraged to taste before you buy and are educated in the process, all in the most friendly and unintimidating atmosphere.[6]

Why does Ken matter this much? Part of it has to do with personal charisma. Ken grew up Polish Catholic and working class, a couple of miles away in Byram, Connecticut. My wife grew up nearby, and she remembers the young Ken as a god—blond, imposing, admired by all. Now in his fifties, he has lost some of the Viking physique but remains handsome and charming. He spends his life striking up conversations with perfect strangers over the counter, coaxing them out of their

New England anomie, and it almost always works. Being this likable, for so many years, with this many people, does something to a man. In Ken's case, it makes him good.

But there's more. Ken is a man on a mission.

Ken started his career in the cheese "industry." This meant selling a product produced at scale, highly processed, ferociously packaged, sometimes barely edible. But in the past few decades, our relationship with cheese, as with so many other foods, has been transformed by what I call the Alice Waters effect, after the woman who did so much to change the way Americans think about food. Now it is more carefully made, in smaller batches, with spectacular improvements in taste and texture. Ken typically works with husband-and-wife teams who keep cows, goats, sheep, even water buffalo. "They make cheese by hand . . . in a time-honored, traditional way, with great integrity to animal husbandry as well as the production of the cheese," Ken told me. This is a preindustrial—actually, anti-industrial—enterprise that is, in Ken's words, "smaller, more crafted, more special."

In effect, Ken has helped bring the artisanal trend to Darien.

He is loved for it. Everyone wants to be current, even people in snooty Darien. The old order in Connecticut was preoccupied with wealth and standing, and cheese was an opportunity to show off a deep knowledge of the finer things, a discriminating palate that says you are a creature of discernment and therefore worthy of your high position. (This is the difference between new money and old money, of course.)

Ken doesn't care about the old order. In fact, he sees his cheese store as a Trojan horse, a way to spirit something into Darien homes. His target is Saturday night. Traditionally, Darienites have used Saturday night to make a quiet but emphatic statement of wealth and standing. Tables glitter with china, crystal, and silver. Homes are beautifully appointed, taste made manifest. What the home doesn't communicate about the occupant's status will often be made explicit over the course of the meal. "Of course, Lawrence is at Choate. And then Yale, we think. Or possibly Princeton. Daniel went to Princeton, didn't you, darling?" Heaven forbid anyone forget that Daniel went to Princeton.

This is the Connecticut so hated in popular culture, the one scorned by writers and filmmakers who made it the home of robotic women (*Stepford Wives*, 1975 and 2004), anti-Semitism (*Gentleman's Agreement*, 1947), and desperate conformity (*The Man in the Gray Flannel Suit*, 1956; *The Ice Storm*, 1997; *Revolutionary Road*, 2008). As an anthropologist, I've always been a little nervous about this portrayal. It's repeated so eagerly it sounds more like myth than criticism. And I would be less suspicious if critics engaged in reciprocal self-criticism. But they don't. This is asymmetric skepticism.

In my conversation with Ken, it became clear that he's not a fan, either. In fact, he hates the idea that his cheese ends up on the status table. "Food was not meant to be treated this way," he says. He's hoping for a different kind of interaction, in which "people just land cheese on the table in the wrapper, open it up, and [say], 'Hey, we've got a great bottle of wine, we've got great food.'" It's not about serving the priciest Bordeaux. It's about "us talking, sharing a good glass of wine together, hanging out. 'We let our kids run around and play in the yard' kind of thing. . . . It's just about enjoying what it is, the beverage, the food, being together, people connecting again."

To say that Ken hopes to transform Darien is not to imply that he's a firebrand, a class champion, a social reformer. Well, maybe he is a social reformer. But there is no evidence that Ken scorns those he would reform. His mission presents as a simple generosity, without class hostility or self-aggrandizement. Ken is a kindhearted saboteur.

I think this helps explain why Ken gets credit that Bob, Jim, and Erin do not. He is helping to transform his community in a way that people in Darien are happy to be transformed. There is a growing consensus that privilege can act as a trap, a gilded cage. For an earlier generation of Darienites, status was the great preoccupation of social life. But for a new generation, the model feels broken—or at least a bit tedious and confining.

Some people are even bailing on Darien. Houses are harder to sell, and people are migrating to towns more like the one I live in. Once happy with giant one-acre lots miles from town, they now want to be able to "walk to town." The old model was separation and distance. Now it's actually making contact, having conversations, knowing your neighbors.

So of course Ken is a hero. His cheese shop was one of the staging areas for this revolution. He is helping people stage-manage that transition from status dinner to conversation around the island. He is helping them move from hierarchy to something closer to community.

Ken is honored for his accomplishments—not with stuffed-shirt ceremony, or plaudits and awards, but his name carries weight. His reputation precedes him. This is a man to be reckoned with. So he is much better "compensated" than Bob, Jim, or Erin. Why? We'll get to that.

## 2.5 Storyteller Drew

Drew is also loved for what she does. Once a week or so, we will go for a long walk. (Walking is one of Rowayton's new passions and was even before COVID-19.) Occasionally someone will pull up beside us, roll down the window, and just beam at her. This never happens to me, I can tell you.

Drew Lamm runs a writing workshop out of her home, called Taste Life Twice. Here's what one of her students said about her:

> Where we live, most people present with such a strong social mask. . . . Everything is perfect and fine and we're happy, ya know. But here [in the workshop], it's real. And in that sense, it's the greatest community. People are really authentic, and it's beautiful.[7]

We can say Drew has something like the effect that Ken does. But her target is less the social world of her students, and more their personal lives.

Another Taste Life Twice student says,

I call her a muse, she has a gift. . . . [T]here is an artistry to how she communicates with each and every one of us in that room. It is so supporting and it's so on target and she doesn't even know how brilliant she is. She reacts with this open heart and this amazing capacity to get the layers underneath what someone has put on the page, that it's really enchanting. And it's very affirming. She's got a touch of magic that she brings to every class.[8]

Drew's home is a little like something out of a storybook. It's surrounded by a wild, unruly garden over which a very tall pine stands sentinel. The house is built into the crest of a hill that supplies the best toboggan run in Rowayton. On snowy days, the house is surrounded by shouts of joy. It has a deep wraparound porch decorated with wind chimes and flowerpots. The inside is lovely, warm, homey, designed to put people at their ease. Drew calls it "funky" and "eclectic."

Drew's workshop is premised on the idea that ordinarily life often rushes past us. But when we write about it, we relive it. We get closer to the meaning of things. Drew's first task is to persuade her students that writing doesn't take any special training or premeditation. "I believe the beauty and craft of literature arrives when you are just writing your stories." Her job is to release a playful spirit. "We all have one," she says in one of her several YouTube videos, "but it gets lost.

We spend so much of our lives giving to other people; our creative selves are yearning to come out."

Drew's workshop encourages people to identify the things in their lives that need seeing and saying. This way lies self-knowledge and self-assertion. Like Ken's work at Darien Cheese, the workshop is a way to let people drop the "social mask" of life in snooty Connecticut—or anywhere, really.

Yes, but why the adoration? Why do we honor Drew and Ken? And not Bob, Jim, or Erin?

Partly, Ken and Drew are visible in a way that Bob, Jim, and Erin are not. The unseen are the unsung. This is one of the things we need to fix.

Also, Ken and Drew are doing more glamorous work. Working on food in a foodie culture, and working on writing in a culture that cares about self-development—these are bound to draw praise.

Finally, it's true that Ken and Drew are working at the top of Maslow's hierarchy. According to this famous theory, some needs rank higher than others. Needs at the bottom are unglamorous: these are the "physiological," "safety," and "belonging." We could call this Hill Top Homes territory. Needs at the top are "transcendence" and "self-actualization"—like expressing oneself through food and writing.

In point of fact, Ken and Drew are getting paid twice. They are seen to be glamorous and then they are well thought of and talked about. Bob, Jim, and Erin, on the other hand, are not getting paid even once. They are not glamorous. They are not praised with notice. This, too, needs thinking about. Don't worry, we'll come back to it.

## CHAPTER 3

# *Honor, an Early Experiment*

In 1588, England feared an invasion by a continental superpower. The Spanish had amassed an armada in the English Channel—130 ships and eighteen thousand men. Her majesty Elizabeth I, Queen of England, should probably have kept to the safety of London or one of her mighty fortifications at Greenwich, Windsor, or Richmond. Instead, she traveled down the Thames to stand in an open field.

She arrived at Tilbury with a bodyguard, but she soon abandoned even this. She rode out to see the troops with a small retinue, a mere handful of people to protect her.

A tiny woman. In plain view. And somewhere very near, the Spanish fleet and, perhaps nearer still, a landing party. Elizabeth had come to defy the Spanish, to declare England indomitable, to insist that an attack on her kingdom must fail.

She spoke.

I know I have the body of a weak, feeble woman; but I have the heart and stomach of a king, and of a king of England too, and think foul scorn that . . . any prince of Europe should dare

---

to invade the borders of my realm; to which rather than any dishonour shall grow by me, I myself will take up arms.[1]

In the sixteenth-century scheme of things, England was little and vulnerable. The troops at Tilbury were hungry, underpaid, and properly terrified. By the Spanish standard, this island was poor, provincial, and home to hundreds of thousands of Catholic sympathizers who had been encouraged to rise up in support of the enemy.

Elizabeth's Tilbury speech was theater in the service of statecraft, infinitely more compelling than the amateur production being staged in the channel by foppish aristocrats firing off conflicting instructions. (The commander of the armada, the Duke of Medina-Sidonia, had never fought at sea.) The Spanish called their armada invincible. Elizabeth had come to Tilbury to say, "No, actually, this is what invincible looks like. My courage will triumph over your titles and grandeur." This is Elizabethan for "Bring it."

It's an irresistible story, one that still speaks to us more than four hundred years later. When Hollywood came to tell the story in *Elizabeth: The Golden Age*, it gave the role of Elizabeth to Cate Blanchett. This was a good idea, given Blanchett's formidable gifts as an actress. But Hollywood then decided to rewrite the Tilbury speech almost entirely.[2]

And this is odd. Surely no scriptwriter could hope to do better than a monarch educated by Roger Ascham in the humanist tradition then flowering in England. But they did. Surely Blanchett could have done something wonderful with "the heart and stomach of a king, and of a king of England too."

But no. What Hollywood writers gave her was pretty much all bombast and testosterone, a lot like Mel Gibson's call to battle in *Braveheart*. In the place of an argument, there is shouting. In the place of performance, there is gesticulation. Poor Ms. Blanchett punctuates her speech with power salutes that Elizabeth would never have used. It is a bleak, stupid moment in an otherwise credible piece of story-telling.

The question is why. Why trifle with Elizabeth's magnificent original speech? Why get it so wrong?

The answer is honor. This idea was at the center of how Elizabeth thought about invasion. She came to Tilbury armed with honor.

> I am come amongst you, as you see, at this time, not for my recreation and disport, but being resolved, in the midst and heat of the battle, to live and die amongst you all; to lay down for my God, and for my kingdom, and my people, my honour and my blood, even in the dust.

We can assume that Hollywood writers looked at this and went, "Huh?" Laying down your blood. That made sense. Sort of. Hollywood could work with that. But laying down your honor. That was, for Hollywood, a puzzler. What was honor anyhow? And how and why would you sacrifice it for your God, your kingdom, and your people? I mean, come on.

No such confusion for the soldiers at Tilbury in 1588. They knew exactly what Elizabeth was saying. For these people, like everyone in

Elizabethan England, honor was an extraordinarily valuable thing. It was a lot like money: a fiction in which everyone believed so resolutely that it served as the lifeblood of a kingdom. It was the measure of standing. (These days we would call it social and cultural capital.) It was a storehouse of value, something you could win or lose, save or squander, and, for a monarch confronted by Spanish ambition, lay down for your God, your kingdom, and your people.

Honor was Elizabeth's way of telling her troops she was all in, that she was prepared to spend the most precious of her resources, that she would stint at nothing. Most of all, she was telling the troops she would reward them.

> I myself will be your general, judge, and rewarder of every one
> of your virtues in the field.

Elizabeth had come to Tilbury to fight Spanish ambition with English honor. She was telling her soldiers she would pay those who fought with her. And she would pay them in the richest of her capitals. Men would rise. Their social status would change. They would leave the field of battle elevated and augmented. Wealthier in material terms. Richer still in honor.

Elizabeth had a lot of honor to work with. Given that she was the highest-ranking person in an acutely hierarchical age, it was fitting that the monarch would have deep reserves. Honor materialized in spectacular ways. Elizabeth had twelve palaces and vast holdings of land and treasure. As monarch she had the right to bestow titles, to elevate people. The ritual might as well have been a kind of magic. Her subjects abased themselves by kneeling before her. With language and gesture, Elizabeth would give them honor. They rose different people. With a few words and a simple ritual, she could make someone *essentially* different.

Monarchs were seen to be honor's point of origin. Honor *sprang* from monarchs. It was theirs to bestow and take back. Elizabeth gave away honor with care and parsimony. This distinguished her from her successor, James VI, who, upon her death, made his way from Scotland, handing out knighthoods with a scandalous generosity. Only those who made themselves particularly useful to Elizabeth could hope for honor. Francis Drake circumnavigated the globe and returned home bearing immense sums of Spanish gold and silver. For this service, Elizabeth made him Sir Francis.

Honor was a liquid thing. It poured from the monarch at the top of the hierarchy and ran downward in a cascade. Think of the "champagne tower" that appears at modern weddings. Glasses are stacked in the shape of a pyramid and filled from the top. Honor moved that way, from high to low, from stage to stage, downward, from monarch to aristocrats, from aristocrats to gentry.

And then it stopped. It stopped where the nation was split asunder, at the boundary separating the court, aristocrats, and gentry and . . . everyone else. The boundary was a barrier honor did not cross. Honor was something you had or didn't have.

Consider the case of Mrs. Moody.

In or around 1582, Mrs. Moody, "upon some suspicion of ill behavior" was sent to prison.[3] Because she was a woman of "good birth and alliance" (i.e., a woman who stood on the high side of the honor boundary), Moody's friends regarded her imprisonment as an outrage and decided to "bust her out," as the modern phrasing would have it.

In the process, they killed a prison guard. When one of the Moody rescuers was arrested for this homicide, the Privy Council (what Americans would call the Cabinet) looked into the matter and decided there was something wrong with sending not just one but two honorable people to prison. Crafting their own version of events, the Privy Council decided the guard had been "transported violently . . . by his own fury." Their finding: the fault was his.[4] This was not homicide. It was self-defense.

The logic here is entirely Elizabethan. Mrs. Moody and her rescuer belonged to the high side of honor and therefore should not be held criminally responsible. Elites were guiltless, even when obviously guilty, and commoners were guilty because, well, they were commoners. Surely any sensible person could see that. Honor was, in this sense, a vicious thing. It could bend reality to its will. It could mint its own truth. It could punish unfairly, and it routinely did.

Yeomen and merchants were a problem of their own. Made prosperous by working the land or the city, they could accumulate a lot of wealth. So much wealth, in fact, they threw the system out of whack. They were living like princes on the non-princely side of the honor boundary. Something had to be done.

A passage into honor had to be constructed. The wealthy yeoman and the merchant had to be elevated. They had to be moved to the high side. There was a system for this. The first step was to engage a herald to examine social origins. Hey presto, the herald would "discover" (often this meant inventing) a distinguished ancestor somewhere in the family tree. In this very English scheme of things, honor was not being created. It was being restored.

This gave the yeoman a coat of arms, and the right to be called a gentleman. But that was just for starters. The rising family was now obliged to spend a fortune on a style of life: the right house, horse, clothing, entertainment, retinue, servants, and self-presentation. (Really, and despite fervent claims to the contrary, the English are the most theatrical people on the face of the earth. This is one reason Shakespeare is their god.)

Elizabethan honor was no merely symbolic thing. It was rooted in the world. It presumed a certain amount of wealth. But wealth by itself was not enough. This wealth was to be very precisely spent. Honor might be an abstraction, but it needed to materialize in exactly the right ways.

The formal position was that it took five generations living correctly to "wash away the taint of commonality." But in fact most families could do it in two or three generations. And if you were really talented, you could do it in one. Thomas Cromwell rose from his beginnings as the son of a Putney blacksmith to become the Earl of Essex. He did this not just in one generation, but in a single decade. (In England, talent could rise in a way it did not in France or Spain, one reason this little nation managed to punch above its weight.)

Honor was many things. It could be used for many purposes. It endowed the individual with many powers. But let's note especially that it provided a kind of freedom. It made you literally the exception to the rule. English social life was strapped this way and that by rules and requirements. Even fashion was constrained. Sumptuary legislation specified who could wear what. If you stood low in the scheme of things, well, tough luck, luxury clothing was not for you. But if you stood high enough, well, sorry for the inconvenience and carry on. All the things prohibited other people were available to you. It's a very English way of doing things. It says to creatures of privilege, *There are rules, but not to worry: they don't apply to you.*

This system is still apparent at the University of Cambridge. No one may walk on certain lawns on college grounds, except for dons who may do so at their pleasure. (This can lead to consternation in the porter's lodge: "*He's* a don?") It appears in a different way in that elitist rule of thumb: never explain, never apologize. Honor sets you free. Rules are for little people. You no longer need exert yourself to satisfy the expectations of others. You are your own arbiter. We will return to this.

Honor was calculable. The average Elizabeth could say how much honor someone possessed through a complicated assessment of service to the throne, number of generations in place, rank and standing of ancestors, source of wealth, amount of wealth, holdings, personal accomplishments, access to the court, local influence, and the kind and place of your education. (There were rich colleges at Cambridge and poor ones.)

It was a complicated business, but a necessary one. Any social event that brought people together to eat at table required that they be seated in exact correspondence to their social standing. This made the seating chart a reproduction of the hierarchy. For John Aubrey, the seventeenth-century diarist, this meant hard service. Family debts and a series of lawsuits forced him to sell his estates and throw himself on the kindness of his family. Now he was their captive at table as they not only chose the topics of conversation but, without the possibility of reproach, droned relentlessly on and on.

Here's one strange thing about honor. It was visible, vivid, and measurable. It was known and pretty much agreed upon. But it was still a very fragile thing. Almost anyone, it turns out, could diminish your honor by "dishonoring" you with an insult. When two parties met in public, the lesser party was obliged to defer to the greater party. This meant "giving them the wall," or letting them pass on the inside. (Given the things Elizabethans threw from upper stories into the street, this was no small benefit.) It meant raising one's hat. It meant bowing and, if need be, scraping. Each of these ritual details was an opportunity for insult. The lesser party could simply refuse to raise his hat. Or he could raise it halfheartedly or, gasp, ironically. It was possible to shade the ritual, withholding just enough deference to provoke the greater party. Then all hell could break loose. By the sixteenth century, duels had largely fallen out of fashion. But sometimes the sensitivities inspired by honor were so tender that an "affair of honor" was impossible to avoid.

Whew. What a complicated thing honor was. There were a lot of moving pieces to this clockwork world. But one single overarching objective was accomplished: everyone sought the same thing, and knew how to get it.

Honor did wonderful things in the Elizabethan world. It created good. It made people responsive to a center. It supplied them with a moral compass. It sent them into service for their queen and her kingdom. It encouraged noble pursuits and discouraged ignoble ones. Honor inspired. Honor improved. Honor elevated.

But for our purposes it is a very bad moral compass. For our purposes, it is too partial, available to some, not to all. Tradition in Elizabeth's age insisted that honor comes from a monarch, when we may wish to fashion honor for ourselves. It throws low-standing people under the bus without a second thought. It is completely captive of a status system that Americans regard as an affront to democratic principle. It allows (and requires) a single public expression. We are more comfortable with variety. Elizabethan honor insisted that it was not honor unless it is manifested in a very particular way. We believe in multiplicity. Honor may have bid Elizabethans care about things that served the public good (or kingdom), but it also made them showy and status sensitive. Sometimes, it made them care about the wrong things and act in the wrong ways.

We will have to keep some things in this code and jettison others. We have our work cut out for us.

## CHAPTER 4

# *American Postcards*

Restoring honor won't be a simple matter of sweeping aside everything that competes against it. Since the days when honor reigned supreme, an extraordinary number of codes and conventions have come and gone. This is, after all, what Americans do: make the rules up as we go along. The American experience is one long experiment, a relentless recasting of who we are.

If honor is to be restored, it will have to find a place for itself in the present sea of cultural and moral innovations. And that's what I want to do here: look at some of the innovations that have shaped and reshaped us. Honor must embrace these, or at least learn to work alongside them.

## 4.1 Meghan & Harry and the Avant-garde

It began so well. Prince Harry met the American beauty Meghan Markle on a blind date in the summer of 2016. They were engaged a year and a half later, and married a year after that. They were now the Duke and Duchess of Sussex.

Then the bombshell. Roughly two years into their storybook existence, Meghan and Harry announced they wished "to step back as 'senior' members of the royal family," and "carve out a progressive new role." The House of Windsor was unhappy. Queen Elizabeth II was surprised. (A monarch should never be surprised.)

There were a number of forces at work here. The princess was uncomfortable with life in the royal fishbowl. The media treated her in a manner that was intrusive and, in some cases, racist. Harry had seen his mother tormented by the press and eventually destroyed by it. Would he allow the media to treat his wife as it had his mother? "Megxit" was perhaps inevitable.

Media aside, Meghan Markle was bound to be unhappy with life in the royal world. She did not warm to the Windsor idea of service, not because she didn't care about doing good works, but because she had her own idea of what good works were. The royal family are tireless supporters of traditional institutions, including the Red Cross, military battalions, museums, and organizations like Badminton England. To Meghan and Harry, these institutions seemed old-fashioned and out of touch. Worse, supporting them required an endless succession of ceremonial events, where the work of the royals was simply to show up and sit there. The Sussexes wanted to take their own initiative in the performance of more demanding work, sometimes in brand-new ways. Where the Windsors were passive, the Sussexes are active.

To make matters worse, the couple was caught between two celebrity systems: the royal family and Hollywood. It's easy to ridicule the comparison. Surely when compared to the House of Windsor, Hollywood is a rash and reckless system that America was obliged to invent only because it had unwisely declined to install monarchs and aristocrats of its own. At least, this is the royal view. The American answer is usually, "Yes, but have you actually seen Charlize Theron act? How about Viola Davis? Our royals make your royals look like a puppet on a stick."

Meghan was an adroit navigator of Hollywood celebrity. She created The Tig, a website that gave lifestyle advice. She used endorsements skillfully. She played the media like a violin. But as a royal, she soon learned, she could no longer practice self-construction and self-direction. There was now no opportunity to maneuver by her own efforts. Everything was pretty much "laid on" by centuries of tradition and a formidable Windsor bureaucracy. Like Diana before her, Meghan faced imposed passivity and the prospect of doing good only by showing up.

But there is a deeper explanation for why Meghan and Harry took their leave. The key, I think, is honor. Megxit was actually the outcome of a contest between the ancient order of honor and a new system that rose to challenge it.

The new system became visible in the middle of the nineteenth century.[1] It was especially evident in Paris, where artists defined themselves in new ways. They saw the middle class and the mainstream as conformist and controlling and themselves as an "avant-garde," rebellious and risk-taking. This encouraged a new cardinal distinction of the Western social world: "in or out." The social world once so abjectly oriented upward was now torn in two, with conformists on the inside and rebels on the outside.

The avant-garde community in Paris was tiny. Their mission was to break the rules of art and life, to "*épater* the bourgeoisie." Living in Montmartre in bohemian chaos was meant to subvert the middle class as much as anything accomplished by one's art. Manet's *The Absinthe Drinker* was designed to scandalize both the salon and the Salon.[2]

From these small beginnings in Paris, the avant-garde movement grew larger and more powerful. Its expansion was aided by the arrival of wealthy Americans, people who didn't actually need to live in garrets, but chose to do so because they loved the look. They grew so numerous, the Latin Quarter was sometimes called the American Quarter.[3] Paris mostly welcomed this inpouring of American wealth, and aristocratic American families were grateful for a place to lodge the "artistic" child.[4]

For all its galleries, dealers, patrons, and museums, the art world is small. The avant-garde needed a bigger audience, and Hemingway's 1926 novel *The Sun Also Rises* gave it one. In hardcover, the message was now available in public libraries; in softcover, it could be found in drugstores.

Hemingway's novel was an instant success.[5] It became a manual for those who would never go to Paris. It supplied "lifestyle" details on how to dress, to live, to speak. It showed how to break the rules of middle-class life even for those who had no artistic inclination.

The avant-garde impulse was still more widespread after World

War II.[6] America saw the arrival of "Beats."[7] The prime mover was William S. Burroughs, who abandoned a life of privilege in St. Louis and a Harvard education for a heroin addiction and destructive self-discovery on Chicago's North Side. This wasn't Montmartre.[8] It was better. Burroughs cared nothing for aesthetic redemption or romantic airs. He styled himself a criminal and worked as a bug exterminator. The boy from upper-class St. Louis had found a home.[9]

Beats, too, protested the bourgeois view of the world. They scorned the tidy and the straitlaced. They sought to destroy conventional ways of seeing and being. Jack Kerouac found spontaneity in Benzedrine, jazz, and "wild form" prose. He criticized Allen Ginsberg for being rule-bound.[10]

The Beats were covered by *Time* and *Life*. As a kid growing up in postwar Vancouver, I first saw them in these magazines, on a middle-class coffee table. The articles had a weird duality: the tone might express official disapproval, but the prose itself was quietly celebratory. Popular culture was mesmerized. So was I.

Another novel rose to carry the avant-garde banner. Kerouac's 1957 book *On the Road* sold extremely well. The novel detailed still more lifestyle instructions, and these were embraced across the US. A resentful Burroughs muttered, "Kerouac opened a million coffee bars and sold a million pairs of Levi's."

The avant-garde impulse was not done. It helped animate the counterculture of the 1960s. Allen Ginsberg befriended Timothy Leary and the Beatles. He was a guiding light of the 1967 Human Be-In in San Francisco, the same city in which Beat poet Lawrence

Ferlinghetti and his bookstore supplied a staging area and essential literature for the hippie revolution. Bob Dylan proved an essential convert. His move from acoustic to electric helped smooth the transition between cultural moments.

Compared to the streetwise hipster who haunted Times Square, hippies were kinder, gentler, starry-eyed. (New drugs, new vistas.) But finally, hippies shared the "madness" Kerouac prized.[11] They violated the middle-class code to a purpose.

But hippies also democratized the avant-garde impulse. To be a hippie, one didn't actually have to make art or music. For many people, it was enough to be young and dress the part. Millions could now participate. And now that music counted more than novels or poetry, you didn't need to know how to read.

Good measures are hard to find, but I extracted some numbers from the "Hippie" entry in Wikipedia.[12] In 1965, there were only a thousand prototypical hippies living in the Bay Area. The next year, this population grew by an order of magnitude. Ten thousand people attended the Trips Festival organized in 1966 by Stewart Brand, Ken Kesey, and Owsley Stanley. By one estimate, there were now fifteen thousand hippies in Haight-Ashbury alone. The following year, 1967, twenty thousand people attended the Human Be-In in San Francisco. This was in January. Clearly the word was out. The meme, so to speak, was launched. That same year, a hundred thousand people came to San Francisco for the "Summer of Love." A couple of years later, five hundred thousand people attended Woodstock. And by the 1970s, millions of young Americans were prepared to call themselves hippies.

Once more, *Time*, that organ of the American middle class, helped tell the story.

> "The standard thing is to feel in the gut that middle-class values are all wrong," says a West Coast hippie. . . . The middle-class ego, to the hippie, is the jacket that makes society straight, and must be destroyed before freedom can be achieved.[13]

Something had changed. *Time* had initially treated the Beats with ambivalence, but their take on hippies was almost respectful. The story, "Youth: The Hippies," gets a dignified cover line ("The Philosophy of a Subculture"), and the content is sympathetic, instructional, in places almost proselytizing.

> If there were a hippie code, it would include these flexible guidelines: Do your own thing, wherever you have to do it and whenever you want. Drop out. Leave society as you have known it. Leave it utterly. Blow the mind of every straight person you can reach. Turn them on, if not to drugs, then to beauty, love, honesty, fun.

So you'd think by this time, after a hundred years of assault by the avant-garde, the middle class would be ready to throw in the towel. Clearly, it was losing the war. As the torch passed from Montmartre to Montparnasse to Chicago to San Francisco, the outsiders were poised to become insiders, defining the mainstream of American culture.

Which brings us back to Meghan and Harry. Their existence appeared charmed, but the Sussexes were in fact the captives of a court society. This is a world before artists, avant-garde writers, Beats, and hippies. This is a world untouched, relatively speaking, by the avant-garde. This is a world of perfect clarities and very defined roles.

As a male, you are defined as a father, son, citizen, subject, employer, employee, soldier, devotee, believer, belonger, adherent. Each of these roles has rules, and the rules are clear (and surprisingly redundant). Royals are a little like Victorians and can reasonably expect people (especially those charged with high office) to deliver a "sincere" performance of these social roles and rules. This means knowing your place in the pageant of royal life and playing your part.

But Meghan and Harry are the creations of a post-court society, one that tends to see roles and rules as falsehoods. They were raised to believe that social conformity could only obscure, if not actually damage, the authenticity of the self. In modern America, people had an assignment: discover the essential self and the authentic moment— and if that meant forsaking roles and rules, well, so be it. As the masterful observer of the twentieth century Lionel Trilling might have observed, the royal court was dedicated to sincerity. The Duke and Duchess believe in authenticity.[14]

Especially Markle. She is a young woman raised in Los Angeles, where the culture of Victorian England was inaudible. She is a product of the West Coast, with all its devout commitments to self-realization. She went to private schools and eventually to Northwestern University. She chose to become an actress, and that meant getting an education focused on finding the "truth" of one's character, not one's social identity.

Like many actresses, Markle was consumed by anxiety. As she now remembers,

> I was in my early 20s, still figuring so much out, and trying to find my value in an industry that judges you on everything that you're not versus everything that you are. Not thin enough, not pretty enough, not ethnic enough, while also being too thin, too ethnic, too pretty the very next day.[15]

Markle's moment of Trillingesque liberation came during a casting call. She was auditioning for a casting director named April Webster. Webster is a Hollywood institution, but she and Markle had never met. Webster stopped Markle mid-scene and said, "You need to know that you're enough. Less makeup, more Meghan."

Markle tells us this "changed everything." This was the beginning of her mission not to please a capricious industry but to express her authentic self. Her website The Tig asked women to craft *their* idea of beauty. Markle wanted to discover her real selfhood, and to help others do the same.

Imagine you are Meghan Markle. You are a product of American culture in several ways. But perhaps most powerfully, you are a person who puts true experience above empty ceremony. And empty ceremony now turns out to be your job. From the outside, life as a princess might have appealed to her (it appeals to millions of Americans), but close up it must have felt burdensome, even like a threat to her essential self.

Markle is, as we all are, a descendant of those Parisian bohemians, American novelists, Beat poets, hippies, punks, and a perennial avant-garde. Naturally, she is inclined, as so many of us are, to heap scorn on roles and rules, and to avoid the "prison house" of bourgeois conformity.[16] To Meghan Markle, the royal family may well have felt like captivity.

The Markle story gives us a glimpse of what honor was up against. In the beginning, honor brought order to the world. It ranked people high and low, and helped govern behavior and supply a moral code. Then came those dreadful Parisians, people who used their art to attack the morality of the mainstream. Suddenly, honor began to look mechanical and slavish. Now you had to choose. Were you going to be conformist and gutless? Or were you going to embrace a more heroic search for selfhood?

## Honor as Something Clueless and Unfashionable

Unfortunately, the aforementioned artists have besmirched honor's good name. They have persuaded us that honor is for the Dudley Do-Rights of the world, for people who crave approval and security. They made honor an object of scorn, something that matters only to people who are incapable of creativity and play. Honor might work for some, but not for Meghan, not for creatives, not for actresses, not for millions of Americans.

Fair enough. In its traditional form, honor is the dead hand of convention, something that threatens to press us into ill-fitting roles and responsibilities. Most of us would be inclined to join with the Sussexes and doubt the value of pageantry. This is the part of the honor code we can do without.

But let's not jettison honor altogether—not yet, at least. Especially when we find ourselves surrounded by a rising tide of bad behavior. It's possible that the shift from sincerity to authenticity, for all its good intentions, damaged our moral compasses.

On its face, honor isn't "cool." No one who values their "street cred" or their claim to cool wants to be seen as a drone, as a conformist. Honor is for the teacher's pet, the kid incapable of cool.

But there is no necessary contradiction here. We are merely saying that whatever we accomplish in the reformation of selfhood, there are some things we still owe to Caesar. Our social life gives us roles as spouses, children, parents, citizens, neighbors. And honor expects us to fulfill those roles.

It's a simple proposition. There are some things we owe to the Christ of self-discovery, and these must not be allowed to obscure what we owe to the Caesar of our social responsibility. So by all means, pursue your essential selfhood. Go "on the road." Write poetry. Figure out who you *really* are. But do not forget what you owe to others. This, too, is part of an essential self.

Charlie Rose perhaps saw himself as someone who needed freedom to pursue his inner intellectual, to discover that he had the heart of an aesthete or the soul of a Scandinavian dramatist. Go for it, Charlie.

But assaulting interns? Charlie's search for himself created a workplace that was, for Sophie Gayter, abusive. The Harvard soccer spreadsheet may have seemed jolly good, perhaps even ironic fun, for those undergraduates, but for Hannah Natanson it was an act of terrorism.

The takeaway is simple. Self-creation, self-expression are good things. We live in an individualistic society. We are charged with the responsibility of figuring out who we are. Only thus can we discover our strengths and deliver them to the rest of us. But anytime we embrace a self-discovery that necessitates the diminishment of someone else, that's when honor must intervene and impose a "cease and desist" order. That's when it is time to cut it out. That's when Charlie Rose is obliged to put on his big-boy pants—or any pants, really—and act with the dignity honor demands of him.

There is one thing that honor can learn from the rise of the avant-garde: the concept of internal honor, which we will talk about at length below. This honor is free to stand outside the conventions of the moment and the middle class, and make its own, deeply personal pact with selfhood.

All in all, the avant-garde inflicted a terrible injury on the honor code. It poured scorn on anything that looks like conformity. It dressed up and celebrated the notion that outsiders were interesting, dangerous, dramatic, and cool. In the process, it unleashed an individualism that happily wreaked havoc on the lives of bystanders. You want bad treatment? Strike up a relationship with an artist. He is duty bound to pursue his truth even if it damages those around him. (Yes, it's usually a "him.") It is almost as if artists believe they have the right to behave badly. After all, it's for their art. And eventually we managed to democratize the artist's freedom. Now we could all treat one another badly.

The honor code we propose here floats on top of all the artist's furious self-invention. We are entitled to embrace that self-invention for ourselves, but certain conditions apply. We have to get a few things right. We need to respect roles, respect our colleagues, respect those who work for us and for whom we work. This is the minimum requirement. After that, we are free to become anyone we like, to engage in all manner of self-invention. As long as we satisfy honor's demands, we are free.

# 4.2 Celebrity Culture

Paging through a newspaper from the first half of the twentieth century, we see a world we have lost. There were spiritual leaders, men and women of science, great writers, gifted athletes, moral exemplars, world explorers, business tycoons, politicians, philanthropists, friends of the poor, champions of the weak.

The present day is different. We admire actors. And . . . and that's it, really. Okay, sure, athletes. And a few others: Oprah, Elon Musk, and um, okay, I give up. Many of the old elites—religious clergy, social elites, business leaders, scientists, community leaders, politicians—have been brought low. But celebrities, we love. You might even say we are obsessed with them.

MIT did a study a few years ago that shows how swiftly this change has taken place. At the turn of the century, actors occupied around 16 percent of public consciousness (as determined by an assessment of contemporary documents). Biologists occupied about 8 percent. Writers came in at 11 percent. By the middle of the century, actors had risen to 24 percent. Writers had fallen to 8 percent. And by the beginning of the twenty-first century, actors were up to a whopping 50 percent, and if you add in singers and musicians, entertainers now controlled a 70 percent share of mind. Writers had fallen to just under 2 percent. (I know.)[17]

Celebrity books dominate the bestseller lists. They are out there pitching their products and their causes. They are the stuff on which Twitter and Instagram run. They dominate TV at prime time with shows like *Entertainment Tonight, Inside Edition, Extra, Access Hollywood*. And they are there to put us to bed at the end of the day, on *Jimmy Kimmel Live!, The Tonight Show Starring Jimmy Fallon, The Late Show with Stephen Colbert, Late Night with Seth Meyers*, and *A Little Late with Lilly Singh*.

Signs of our celebrity-centricity are everywhere. Take Matthew McConaughey. Type "Mcconaughey" into a Word or Pages document. Did the software correct you? Of course it did. That's what it is to live in a celebrity culture. Even our software wants to honor our gods. Because, hey, Matthew matters.

Much of the celebrity coverage is addled. Questions are exercises in flattery. "Here's a question that has always troubled me," asks the host. "Would you say you are 'astonishingly wonderful' or 'utterly fabulous'?" The celebrity is treated with the utmost deference. We don't learn much of anything except that the celebrity really, really loves his wife, his children, and all the actors he has ever worked with. The journalist effectively acts as a PR agent or studio hack.

It is customary to suggest that this passion for celebrity culture is a clear sign of our senescence, the twilight of our gods, and/or the end of everything serious and substantial in our culture. Preening intellectuals, often looking for celebrity of their own, are censorious. Daniel Boorstin complained that American culture was a place in which people could be famous merely for being famous. This is actually wrong, but the assertion made Boorstin very famous. Christopher Lasch thought he detected an epidemic of narcissism. We were all in love with ourselves.[18] (He may have been onto something here.)

There is no doubt that a celebrity culture encourages empty fame and self-absorption. But it also speaks to some of the fundamentals of the American experience.

For starters, there's an obvious reason we love celebrity. These people are beautiful, charming, and talented, and (generally) they use these qualities in a skillful way to make themselves as agreeable as possible. What's not to like? (Well, except for the self-absorption and self-promotion.) These people are not famous for being famous. They are famous for being ever so appealing.

Plus, we spend a lot of time with these people. On average, we see five movies a year in the theater. We watch five hours of TV a day. We follow celebrities on Instagram. It's bound to have an effect. We know some of these people at least as well as we know our friends, maybe even members of our families.

We love to marvel at the grandeur of these lives. It's grist for the fantasy mill. And when that isn't enough, they indulge our schadenfreude. We notice when they fail. And they fail a lot. Let the record show: Lil Peep, Heath Ledger, Britney Spears, Kathy Griffin, Demi Lovato, and Shia LaBeouf.

In spite of these sometimes tragic outcomes, celebrities supply some people with what we might call life advice. The young man who is casting about to define his maleness (no easy task these days) may choose from the action-hero resoluteness of a Tom Cruise, the complexity of a Clive Owen, the satiric edge of a Ryan Reynolds, the ironic detachment of a Ryan Gosling, the tough-guy athleticism of a Mark Wahlberg, or the controlled ferocity of a Christian Bale. Celebrities help us define ourselves. They supply identities.

Celebrities now help script our lives. Twenty years ago, I was living in Montreal, and I decided one night to go looking for the ghost of Mordecai Richler, Canada's gift to the twentieth-century novel. I was quizzing the bartender at Winnie's, his favorite bar, and the door flew open. And a man entered, shouting, "Yeah, baby!"

Everyone got the reference. It was November 2002 and "Yeah, baby" was everywhere, thanks to Mike Myers and his character Austin Powers. Hollywood creates phrases, and these then become fixtures of our social life: "What's up," "Too much information," "Don't go there," "That's why they pay him the big bucks," "Say my name," "You can't handle the truth," "You go, girl," "You think?," "D'oh," "It doesn't get any better than this," "Winter is coming," "I have a very particular set of skills," "Good times," "My precious," "Did I say that out loud?" The last was first uttered by Cliff Clavin on *Cheers* and still circulates many years later. A last example: the "woo" sound made by "woo girls" and featured on *How I Met Your Mother*.[19] Celebrities are not just entertaining us, they are scripting our social performances.

I went to my dermatologist recently, and I found myself staring at ads for tummy tucks, skin resurfacing, cool sculpting, fillers, Botox for young people. If you were a visitor from outer space and this office was the only thing you knew about us, you would say that we were a culture obsessed with chasing a dragon called youth.

When I got home, I looked up the stats. In the US, there were around three hundred thousand breast augmentation surgeries in 2018; 250,000 liposuctions; and two hundred thousand nose reshapings. Botox was responsible for 7.4 million procedures. There were over a million chemical peels. More than 80 percent of Americans whiten their teeth. Nearly six hundred thousand got veneers in 2006.[20] Not all of this work is being done in imitation of our celebrity betters. I don't think. Oh, wait. I stand corrected. It is. Celebrities are shaping our bodies.

Our adoration of celebrity culture goes deeper still. A couple of months ago, I did a study of young women in their twenties. The question was, what did they do to amuse themselves on the weekend, and especially on a Saturday night? The answer was surprising. These women told me that they would spend a long time getting ready to go out, sometimes a couple of hours. And then they thought hard about whom they wanted to see and how things would go. On the occasion itself, women were looking for the usual things: fun, excitement, romance.

They were also hoping to turn in a great performance.

"What?" I asked in my smooth manner. "Huh?" One respondent told me she couldn't be sure she'd had a good time until she had a chance to look at Instagram the next day. These photos would tell the tale. Did she look fabulous? Did she look riveting? Did she look like a celebrity? (I looked at the Instagram record in question and a lot of them did.)

I wondered if this was a limited phenomenon—after all, all the women I spoke to lived nearby. And then I stumbled on some statistical data that suggest otherwise. Alcohol consumption is going down for people in their twenties. The reason? Instagram. No one wants to be caught drooling in front of the camera. Because Insta is forever. Or, as one of them put it, "Look, I can't afford a bad photo on Instagram. Drunk and stupid looking? Please. That could ruin me."

This performance culture, the one in which we celebrate our celebrities, marks a change. Some years ago, Tom Peters wrote an essay on "brand you."[21] He encouraged readers to think about themselves as brands and to market themselves accordingly. Look, he said, your employer no longer cares about you in the long term. You are disposable. This was the 1990s, and a generation of people went, "Right. Time to brand myself."

Almost twenty-five years later, the mantra has changed. "Brand you" has become "celebrity me." This is the strategic way to fight off obscurity and build a more lasting public profile. "Celebrity me" is, for some, a way to craft a social self.

It's worth pointing out the downside. Constructing a "celebrity me" and then communicating this through the right social channels with the right social strategies is hard work. Lilly Singh started modestly, with a few performances on YouTube, and soon became one of the most popular stars there. But in 2018, she hit a wall. "I'm gonna be real with y'all: I am mentally, physically, emotionally, and spiritually exhausted."[22] Her fellow YouTube celebrity PewDiePie said, "You realize you can't take a break, because if you take a break your numbers will fall. And if your numbers go down, people notice that you're failing and not doing as well. . . . You're stuck constantly producing content." Social is a beast. It must be fed constantly. Or people will "notice you're failing." We imitate celebrities even when our exertions can cost us dearly.

Ours is an individualistic culture. Our life mission will depend on how we craft ourselves. And our life chances will be determined by how attractive and persuasive we have made ourselves. Celebrities serve as exemplars. They help us contemplate some of our existential options.

So, useful as it may be for some purposes, celebrity culture interferes with honor. It doesn't care about what Bob, Jim, and Erin do. Bob is merely some guy who volunteers around town. Erin works at the gardening club. They may have shaped our little town, but celebrity culture doesn't care. There isn't enough beauty, charisma, or red carpet here. Worse, celebrity exalts some people who are monsters of vanity. It asks us to pay attention not to accomplishments, but to surfaces. In a celebrity culture, you can be dissolute, even abusive, but as long as your Instagram feed looks nice, you are good to go.

The ascent of celebrity culture supplanted honor. It obscured the needs of a Hill Top Homes or of hungry children. As we have seen, it is not entirely superficial. People can take real inspiration and comfort from celebrities. But nothing in the celebrity self urges us to do for others, to commit ourselves to something larger than ourselves.

As you can see, I am taking pains to avoid the argument that says celebrity culture is all empty self-indulgence. This argument has inflicted huge damage to our self-understanding. The enemy here, it turns out, is not celebrities, but the constant din of criticism that rolls off the university presses as intellectuals, clueless in their understanding of contemporary culture, can't wait to stand in judgment of it. We have to reckon with why celebs matter. Repudiation is not possible. It is not wise.

What we are trying to do here is to bolt honor on top of everything we do in American culture and hope this has the effect of giving us a moral compass and a path to goodness. Honor comes from service. It comes from accomplishment. Honor is a jealous god. It says we should care about something larger than ourselves.

The good news is that we may be entering a period of celebrity fatigue. Madonna was recently asked to give a tribute to Aretha Franklin, and she spoke mostly about herself. The audience was stunned, and social media dared to ridicule her. *Slate* offered an essay titled "Madonna's Eurovision Performance Somehow Fails to Solve Israeli-Palestinian Conflict."

But it's not just Madonna who's on the firing line. Ricky Gervais is routinely hired to roast celebrities, and he's made #hollywoodhypocrites a trending hashtag. In his parody, *In the Time It Takes to Get There*, Zach Braff shows the vacuity of the new influencer celebrity.[23] The

*New York Times* excoriated an effort by celebrities to give comfort by singing a version of "Imagine."[24]

Perhaps this is the beginning of a celebrity culture in decline.[25] Perhaps celebrity and honor will pass one another, as one falls and the other rises.

# 4.3 Swift Selves

After World War II, America witnessed an economic expansion of unimaginable proportions. People had been deprived for much of the first half of the twentieth century, suffering world wars, depression, shortages, and rationing. By the end of the Second World War, they were ready for the century to start (already). This is what economists call pent-up demand.

A hyperbolic economy ensued. People were moving out of the city into new suburbs, which meant homes had to be constructed and furnished. That icebox that had served three generations in a Brooklyn walk-up was not welcome on the voyage. What people wanted was a shiny new Frigidaire, to say nothing of a new TV, hi-fi, and stove, plus drapes, rugs, bedding, furniture, art, plates, cutlery, utensils, and decorations. These had to be manufactured, transported, and installed, and America had yet to outsource production to China, so this meant millions of blue-collar jobs. And it all had to be invented, designed, marketed, and sold, which meant millions of white-collar jobs.

Unless locked out of this prosperity by prejudice—and many were, of course—people were prospering. Looking back, my father said to me, "We thought we were working hard, but in an economy like that, how could you fail to do well?"[26]

Strange things happened to food, as all of the new industrial capability developed for the war effort was applied to the home front instead. Corner markets gave way to supermarkets. Food that used to travel in from the countryside by truck now made the journey via assembly line. Food was being prepared, preserved, and packaged in new ways. Remember Sugar Pops (1950), Sugar Frosted Flakes (1952), Swanson TV dinners (1953), Trix (1954), Cocoa Puffs (1956), Tang (1957), and Rice-a-Roni (1958)? This food was now "shelf ready." It was "shelf stable." It was whipped and smoothed. It was salted and sweetened. It was adulterated and preserved, in some cases almost unrecognizably alienated from its natural state.

In the view of the 1950s consumer, this made it better. Wrapped in a radiant package, held up to heaven by an invisible plinth, lit by thousands of watts of fluorescent lighting, it was glorious, pristine, immaculate. Whatever its effect on the actual food, this process of industrialization was very good for the economy. Food in its natural condition makes money only for the farmer and the market. Processed food brought wealth to all the intermediate players.

Food was also made transportable, transformed for people "on the go." Many fast food brands emerged: Dunkin' Donuts (1950), Kentucky Fried Chicken (1952), Denny's (1953), Sonic (1953), Burger King (1954), and McDonald's (1955). This was convenience food, as if speed of access was much—if not the whole—of the point of eating. But of course in a culture dedicated to people "on the go," it was.

People living in the 1950s may have been prosperous, but they were not healthy. For reasons now lost in the mists of time, they would spend one or two weeks a year at a resort where they were baked by the sun, soaked in chlorine, coated in nicotine, and then stuffed with (and like) foie gras. Most of them survived this nutritional nightmare, but in the long term, many paid for it. This was the risk—and, oddly, the reward—of life in the '50s.

Careers were accelerating. People were seeking promotions and getting them. Americans were cultivating "swift selves."[27] We catch a glimpse of this world in the TV show *Mad Men*. For all but the pathetic few, it seemed impossible not to flourish, not to get ahead in the world, not to keep up with the Joneses. In fact, keep up with the Joneses? You wanted to *smoke* the Joneses. You wanted to render them speechless with envy. *Behold our new 1956 Chevy, Admiral TV, Formica counters, and mid-century modern design motifs.* This conspicuous consumption was competitive consumption.

Swift selves came out of the suburbs in one seamless motion. Brand-new homes there served as launching pads designed to fire children into still more exalted social spaces. You fitted your kids with ambitions. You gave them good educations. You asked them not to sit too close to the TV. And you did this under withering fire. Intellectuals and artists called you "bridge and tunnel." John Kenneth Galbraith, Dwight Macdonald, Paul Goodman, and C. Wright Mills openly scorned you.

The suburbs hated this treatment. The protagonist in John Chee-ver's 1969 novel *Bullet Park* says, "[I]t makes me sore to have people always chopping at the suburbs."[28] But they deferred to it. As Donald Katz demonstrates so beautifully in his master ethnography, *Home Fires* (1992), Americans were taking this criticism thoroughly to heart.[29] Those kids raised on a launching pad couldn't wait to become hippies. But for a brief moment after World War II, swift selves were trium-phant.

Increasingly the motif was motion, a relentless upward movement. It was especially evident in the cars of the 1950s.[30] Car designers began to use plane imagery, especially the fighter jet. The names for new models followed suit: Pontiac Strato Star, Hudson Jet, Oldsmobile Rocket. Hood ornaments took the shape of a plane. Even the Packard model called the Clipper had a plane on its hood.

*Time* magazine said, "[M]any new cars borrowed from the shape of swept-wing aircraft to give autos a jet-propelled look."[31] Oldsmobile's ads refer to "new Jetaway hydra-matic," "starfire styling," and "rocket engine." In a moment of candor, a Buick ad admitted, "True, this Buick won't fly—but it does have variable pitch propellers in its Dynaflow Drive." A second Buick ad was called "Flight into Anywhere," and it promised the "untroubled soaring ecstasy of graceful flight."[32]

---

People were struggling to make themselves more aerodynamic, to be sleek and fast. They wanted to be swift. The swift self defines itself by rushing into the world, away from the connections and obligations that define an individual in a traditional society. Such selves sought release from domestic, social, and other constraints.[33] Saul Bellow said,

> For a Midwesterner, the son of immigrant parents, I recognized at an early age that I was called upon to decide for myself to what extent my Jewish origins, my surroundings (the accidental circumstances of Chicago), my schooling, were to be allowed to determine the course of my life. I did not intend to be wholly dependent on history and culture.[34]

The swift self stripped away origins and traditions. It sought to be without encumbrance. It was designed to get things done. It was driven by purpose. It made itself a means to an end. It flourished in the corporation of the second half of the twentieth century; indeed, it was almost perfectly suited to that environment.[35]

Swift selves were pragmatic. They were happy to adapt themselves to the task at hand. They were not surprised or affronted when the organization decided to put someone in their place. They did not believe that their value came from their uniqueness as individuals or the distinctness of the self. They were prepared to conform to the demands of the role. They were prepared to be seen as substitutable.[36]

Many people with swift selves believed their suspension of the self was temporary. Eventually, they thought, the enterprise would pay out, a career would mature, rewards would come. But, sometimes, perhaps often, this was a lie.

When motion defines you, what you fear most is stasis. Swift selves were happiest when in motion. They didn't want ever to "arrive." The pleasure of this self lay precisely in its momentum, the bracing sense of power and safety that comes from being "on the move."

But as a result, there is something tragic about the swift self. At its worst, the swift self suspects there is no stopping, only failing. Swift selves rarely end with grace.

Partisans, boosters, can-do enthusiasts, go-getters, self-help writers, the Tony Robbinses of the world, all celebrate the swift self. They argue that it is nearly impossible to be a productive academic, lawyer, engineer, doctor, or civil servant without being relentless, adaptable, durable, self-monitoring, and creative in just the way that swift selves are. This, they say, is the reason for achievers' constant motion. This is what makes them essential to corporations and to society, both of which are constantly changing and adapting.

This was a new kind of selfhood fit for the twentieth century, and it raised lots of questions. How much could these people take before mental fatigue set in? What were the limits of human endurance when committed to flight in social and professional space? We found out, of course. The incidence of human misery, especially in the form of alcohol addiction and family abuse, was staggering.

But one of the less conspicuous losses was honor. It was not deliberately got rid of; it merely slipped into obscurity. After all, honor was old-fashioned, fusty, the preoccupation of ancient institutions, the very thing we were trying to escape. Instead, we set a course for a bright new future. Swift selves were designed to do important things. And indeed, we must admire their accomplishments: the space programs, universities, social programs, and corporations. But a swift self never gave a second thought to honor.

Honor has a memory. It is historically rooted. It is accumulative. The swift conviction that everything falls away, that nothing sticks, is ultimately wrong. And the idea that we should always get out ahead of tradition and convention is ill-advised. Honor abhors this thinking.

The new honor code we are proposing does not care about lineage, ancestry, or status past. But it does want us to acknowledge that some things stick, that we can't walk away from crimes or misdemeanors. When swift selves rush out of the present into a bright, glorious future, they forget themselves. Honor wants us to remember.

The dawn of the swift self completed our societal shift toward individualism. It separated the individual from previous loyalties. It extracted the individual from larger social contexts, the ones supplied by family, community, nationality. So delineated, the individual was now unmistakably responsible for everything he did. There was no place to hide.

## 4.4 Hippies, Then Preppies

The hippie movement was complicated. There were many causes: the rise of a new generation, indulged by an expansive economy, threatened by military service, struggling to get out from under their parents' "greatest generation," and persuaded of the necessity and the virtue of altered consciousness, sexual freedom, social equality, and cultural experimentation. There were many threads, some British, some American, some folksy, some electronic, some urban, some rural, some stylistic, some anti-stylistic, with other movements— free speech, Black power, anti-war, civil rights, anti-tech—shouting encouragement or at least establishing precedent; additionally, there was an explosion of new ideas about human spirituality and human potential.

> [D]uring the 1960s, a time of accelerating social change driven in part by 42 million Baby Boomers coming of age, Tolkien's *The Hobbit* and *Lord of the Rings* became required reading for the nascent counterculture, devoured simultaneously by students, artists, writers, rock bands and other agents of cultural change. The slogans "Frodo Lives" and "Gandalf for President" festooned subway stations worldwide as graffiti.[37]

There were several reasons to be a hippie, several ways of being a hippie, and several degrees of commitment. You could be living in a Haight-Ashbury commune, experimenting with drugs, free love, shared wealth, and open decision-making. Or you could be a kid living in the American Midwest who was growing his hair, had just bought his first Jimi Hendrix album, and was wondering for the first time whether a career in the insurance industry was really what he wanted to do with his life. The movement was surprisingly inclusive. Even "beginners" were welcome.

In a sense, hippies were on a mission to save swift selves from the inevitable ravages of life in the fast lane. Hippies removed themselves from the preoccupations of status systems, the constraints of corporate life, and the moral bankruptcies of suburban life. Here, finally, was a moral life.

For all its variation, there was an emerging consensus that gave shape and form to the movement. Generally speaking, hippies were egalitarian, rural (if possible), and opposed to capitalism, competition, organized sports, organized religion, and organized crime. They were keen on self-sufficiency, growing their own sprouts, weaving their own cloth, and making attractive, dancing curtains out of threaded corks. They were mystical, skeptical of mainstream ideas, and more or less credulous of anything oddball or alternative. Here's one idea that circulated, to the horror of the medical community: the concept that the human body is a collection of chemicals, and that adding a few more chemicals in the form of hallucinogens was an unexceptional thing to do and almost certainly harmless. There was a strong sense that human beings were perfectible, that the social world could be made utopian, and that if we could just get out from under the harness of the military-industrial complex, goodness must surely flourish. Jean-Jacques Rousseau got a good hearing in the 1960s. His revelation on the road to Vincennes was repeated with admiration and conviction: "Man was born free but lives everywhere in chains." The very point of the '60s was throwing off those chains, in politics, culture, economics, and private life.

Any movement so shot through with experiment, risk, credulity, and optimism was cruising for a bruising. And hippies got one. But by the end of the 1970s, the bills had come due. The rates of drug addiction, depression, suicide, homelessness, even criminality were high.

The world was littered with the movement's "empties." A small New England college hoped to stage a reunion, but discovered that almost everyone in the class of 1976 had met with a premature (in some cases grisly) end. Like the Maoist revolution an ocean away, this revolution ended for many in failure and misery.

We could call it, as historian Gertrude Himmelfarb suggested, the second paradox of liberalism. (The first is that capitalism encourages behaviors that threaten to undermine the foundation of individual liberty.[38]) And this is that when we release people from the social constraints of social role, they tend to treat one another worse, not better. This paradox applies most precisely to hippies. Communes that had been established to plumb the depths of human goodness turned out, in some cases, to be laboratories of pathological behavior.[39]

Eventually, the movement stood with its head bowed. It awaited a large counterreaction to put it out of its misery.

The Antichrist proved to be a kid called Doug Kenney. Kenney went to Harvard in 1964. And he watched as most people on campus began to abandon themselves to all the barefooted excesses of the decade. Doug thought them ridiculous, unsophisticated, artless, and naive. He said so in a book called *Bored of the Rings*, his reply to that most sacred text of the hippie canon, *Lord of the Rings*. This was an easy target for this kid who styled himself the perfect WASP prince. Kenney was just getting started. Over the next few years, he managed a succession of victories, especially the magazine *National Lampoon* and the movie *Animal House*. These held hippies up to scorn.

Kenney had a brilliant parlor trick, one he would perform in your dorm room if you let him.[40] He would turn up, choose a book at random from your bookshelf, and begin reading. At some point, Kenney would begin to make up the text he was "reading." And at some further point, he would put the book down and look at you. Your job was to decide where in the passage the original had stopped and Kenney had begun. Almost no one could. He was that good.

*Bored of the Rings* was Kenney's reply to hippie sincerity. His parlor trick said anyone could do it. Even Kenney. In real time. As you listened. Undetectably. Not art at all, really. Just a liquid and powerful intelligence. Perhaps this is why he found hippies so pointlessly, droolingly earnest. The life was a lie. (Twice a lie, actually.) The mysterious was really the banal. Kenney pressed a question: Who cares if "Frodo lives"?

In a way, hippies had it coming. They were naive. And they were corrupt. Sometimes both. They said that if your heart was in the right place, you could do just about anything and remain above reproach. The hippie ethos was a recipe for excuse-making. Women in the counterculture couldn't help noticing that for all their grand talk of egalitarianism, men were rarely willing to make meals or clean up afterward. Apparently, being part of the vanguard meant never having to say you were sorry.

By the early 1980s, the movement was dying. Preppies were ascendant. Thanks to Kenney, among others, preppies were defining themselves by a simple act of repudiation. They were everything hippies loathed. They were careerist, centrist, class sensitive, and unapologetically hierarchical.

Kenney might have been an enemy of hippies, but he was no friend of honor. His restoration of status, hierarchy, and standing looked a little Elizabethan, but there was nothing here that spoke to a higher calling. Preps were too cynical for that. They wanted you to stop mooning around and take your place in the world. They wanted you to "snap out of it" and "get a life." That last phrase came from David Letterman, head prep. Hippies hoped to break free from bourgeois chains. Dave was more interested in standing in a window of Rockefeller Center reassuring passers that he wasn't "wearing any pants." Funny, vulgar, and a little alarming: the wit that defined the heartless frat bro.

Honor seeks a truth somewhere between the earnest hippie and the cynical preppy. It wants people to hear and embrace a higher calling. But it also wants to embrace preppie realism and world-weariness. Idealistic *and* realistic, that's the thing. Honor holds that human goodness should never be assumed—this is why we need honor as armor.

Hippies helped make important cultural discoveries. That's clear. But they also built up an impressive résumé of bad decisions: the naïveté, the SETI search for new forms of life, the Romantic posturing, the surrender of selfhood and responsibility, the indulgence in drugs, cults, and communes. Without honor as a copilot, this experiment was destined to fail.

This is not to say honor wishes us to commit ourselves to the hair shirt of strict conservatism. We don't want to end up only censorious, constrained by a moral code that's mostly don'ts with precious few dos. I got to know a fellow student at the University of Chicago. He was a student of Allan Bloom and an advocate of the ideas most of us know from

Bloom's book *The Closing of the American Mind*. The guy was brilliant and formidable, and, in a weird way, I was thrilled to see how he chewed through my naive ideas like an industrial-scale wood chipper. But boy, was he angry. His world was tiny and miserable. He was right in some ways, but what cost wisdom? Young fogies, as they came to be called, paid dearly. They won the intellectual battle and lost the existential war.

We want a code that allows us to participate in the culture around us, that allows us to push the American experiment, to investigate the new possibilities out there. We want to have a passport to several worlds, not to a single joyless fogeydom. Honor serves here beautifully. It gives us a light, portable moral code that keeps us centered even as we lean into this new experiment or nimbly away from that one. Our morality can't cost us our mobility. And honor is happy to be our "plus-one."

## 4.5 Artisans

Lift up the industrial layer of the American economy, and underneath are millions of small enterprises, working away, remaking the world. Some 53 million people, fully a third of the workforce, fall into the category of "freelancer." How many are artisans? We don't know. But there's a migration under way.

Artisans matter to us because they help craft some of the material conditions we need to make an honor culture flourish.

There are many ways of being an artisan. We can make beer, beef jerky, bicycles, books, buildings, candy, cheese, clothing, cosmetics, furniture, honey, jam, jewelry, pickles, sausages, soap, kombucha, soft drinks, soup, watches, or whiskey. We can run a farm, a farmer's market, a coffeehouse, a cheese store, or a food truck. At the limit, we can run a tiny taxi company with the help of Lyft, or a tiny hotel thanks to Airbnb.

We can make this an expression of DIY, art, punk, design, folk, or craft. We can do it to "fight the man," destroy consumerism, save the environment, build a kinder, gentler world, reinvent the community, or re/make a life. (We can even do it to prepare for the Zombie Apocalypse.) We can do it as a refusal of the digital world, to make a place that's tangible and manual. We can do it as a part-time gig or a full-time thing. But in all of these cases, we help make our "society of strangers" a place in which honor can emerge and endure as a personal accomplishment.

The Institute of the Future says,

The coming decade will see continuing economic transformation and the emergence of a new artisan economy. Many of the new artisans will be small and personal businesses—merchant-craftspeople producing one of a kind or limited runs of specialty goods for an increasingly large pool of customers seeking unique, customized, or niche products. These businesses will attract and retain craftspeople, artists, and engineers looking for the opportunity to build and create new products and markets.[41]

## Rise of Prepared Food

**1950**
- Sugar Pops
- Minute Rice

**1951**
- Ore-Ida Foods
- Duncan Hines Cake Mix
- Tropicana Products

**1952**
- Sugar Frosted Flakes
- Dehydrated Onion Soup Mix

**1953**
- Sugar Smacks
- Cheez Whiz
- TV Dinners

**1954**
- Butterball Turkey
- Stouffer's Frozen Meals

**1957**
- Pillsbury Cookie Dough

**1958**
- Tang
- Rice-a-Roni
- Sweet'n Low
- Cocoa Puffs

**1959**
- Royal Crown Cola
- Frosty O's

This was true before the advent of the COVID-19 era. And will be still more true after. The industrial piece of capitalism is losing some of its prestige and influence. Once great, grand, and often immaculate, the industrial piece threatens to represent the "back office," the "infrastructure," the mere "offshore supplier" of capitalism. Increasingly, our markets want to show an artisanal face.

Human-scale, handmade, raw or at least unadulterated, unbranded or small-branded, personalized, authentic, simple, local, driven by mission and purpose, defined by story and made and sold by someone you know (or at least know of), creator of social value:

this is roughly what we ask of the artisanal. In the process, we make the social world a more intimate place and honor a more likely outcome.

Boomers were raised on their own planet. They grew up consuming Tang, Kraft macaroni and cheese, Cheez Whiz, Old South orange juice concentrate from the freezer, cakes made from Betty Crocker or Duncan Hines cake mix from a box, and chili made using canned Manwich sauce, not to mention Minute rice, Swanson TV dinners, Pillsbury dough, and Rice-a-Roni. Processed food in the home was mirrored by fast food on the road. Burger King, McDonald's, Kentucky Fried Chicken, and Pizza Hut were all created in the 1950s. This was the Cambrian Era of fast and prepared food.

The pushback came eventually, but it started small. Hippies in the '60s, mostly on the West Coast, began eating things like bean sprouts and brown rice. This was not enough to change the world. Getting lots of people into a big muddy field with a large sound system and lots of drugs, this hippies could do. Creating cultural change that would reach into the heart of a consumer society and transform it— someone else would have to do this.

That someone, in fact, was Alice Waters, who in 1971 started a restaurant in Berkeley, California, called Chez Panisse.[42] It ended up being more than a restaurant—it was a proof of artisanal concept, a philosophical center, a place to train a diaspora of chefs, and eventually the North Star of a movement that would transform food, drink, and eventually both American homes and American markets. Waters and company took an emerging approach to food and gave it new form, power, and efficacy. Put it this way: hippies were reaction; Waters was reform. Or, as the celebrated writer (and Chez Panisse patron) Greil Marcus said of the distinction between hippies in San Francisco and the Chez Panisse crowd across the bay: "We were thinkers; they were crazy."[43]

Things stayed small for quite a long time. Then came the establishment of Chez Panisse in 1971. Except in the food world, the experiment remains obscure. Suddenly, nearly a decade later, the food press wakes up and picks up the Chez Panisse signal. In 1981, *Newsweek* heralded the "Chez Panisse revolution in American cooking." In 1984, the *New York Times* called Alice Waters the force who was "revolutionizing American cooking in the 1970s and 1980s."[44] By the 1990s, Chez Panisse was routinely getting "restaurant of the year" honors. Thus a movement was born.

All of this was happening in the slipstream high up in American culture, the place where fashionable innovations, created by a cultural cognoscenti, pour through the world without ever finding their way to earth, into the lives of ordinary people (by which I mean you and me—okay, me). The innovations that do survive to enter American culture must run an initial gauntlet of popular scorn. Surely, people ask, this exquisite new fashion is just a little too exquisite? People feel threatened by the innovation. It's so strange and new. And they feel insulted that their judgment should be, implicitly, found wanting.

"And what," I believe I must have shouted at some point, "is wrong with TV dinners?"

But eventually, the little trend works its way into the world. In the case of the trend spawned by Waters and Chez Panisse, some of this depended upon the transformation of "health food" into "healthy food." For a long while, food that stood outside the industrial regime, outside the processing system, food that was relatively raw and un-transformed, could only be found in farmer's markets and health food stores. The latter were often disagreeable, apparently disreputable little shops, places so alternative that you would not be surprised to learn they also distributed Marxist-Leninist pamphlets and pornographic literature. This was the wild side of American culture, located inevitably in the wrong part of town in every sense of the phrase. "Health food" was the domain of kooks.

At this moment in American culture, health food was held captive by people who made it more forbidding, not less. One of these was James Edward Baker. Baker served as a marine, a Hollywood stunt-man, and a Vedantic monk, and eventually changed his name to Father Yod. According to a woman called Isis Aquarian, Yod was reupted to have had fourteen wives.[45] In 1969, he founded the Source restaurant in Los Angeles. The food was organic and vegetarian, and the restau-rant was heavily patronized by Hollywood celebrities and local hip-pies. Here's the sign for the place.

No doubt this sort of thing spoke to people entertaining counter-cultural ideas in the 1970s, but certainly most people would have found it odd, even forbidding. Indeed, the sign appears to be deliberately arcane. The upper circle is the reverse of the Great Seal of the United States, but you'd have to be Dan Brown to hazard a guess about its meaning. The symbols along the bottom? Not even Dan Brown can tell us.

Father Yod and his followers were a refreshing corrective to the happy talk of Madison Avenue and Big Food branding. But it wasn't much of an alternative. Father Yod and the Source were not of this world, and for those who were, Yod was a little scary. He confirmed everyone's worst suspicions when, with no training or experience, he decided to go hang gliding off a 1,300-foot cliff in Hawaii. He died nine hours later.

To win favor with a broader audience and diffuse through the American consumer society, health food would have to be de-kookified and rendered harmless. It would have to be made mainstream. At the high end, much of the credit belongs to Alice Waters, who managed to gentrify health food by infusing it with her deep knowledge and love of French cuisine. In the upper middle, the credit goes largely to Whole Foods. Founded in 1980, and scaling up at an astonishing speed, this operation was the perfect opposite of the grimy little health food store. It was airy, light, and un-dubious. Whole Foods managed to eliminate the cultural baggage created by hippies. We could now change our eating habits without changing our political beliefs or style of life. Kenney was especially pleased to learn that he could take to a new style of eating without actually having to keep goats.

Perhaps the best measure of the speed and extent of the artisanal penetration of American culture comes with the arrival of a new species of fast food called "fast casual," exemplified by places like Chipotle (1993), Panera (1999), and Shake Shack (2004). Fast casual takes off.

———

Another measure of the Alice Waters revolution was the transformation of Brooklyn. An influx of artists came to the borough in the 1990s fleeing Manhattan rents. But what started as a Manhattan "outpost" grew eventually into an alternative Manhattan. Brooklyn was Manhattan reimagined. At the center was a new model of production and consumption. The organizing idea, the rallying cry, the magic words: *artisan* and *artisanal*. The borough quickly became a laboratory out of which poured a Cambrian profusion of artisanal brands and products: Mast Brothers chocolate, Grady's Cold Brew, Brooklyn Brine Co. Hop-Pickle, Early Bird granola, Kings County jerky, Brooklyn Salsa Company, Salvatore Bklyn, White Moustache yogurt, Kings County Distillery. The proliferation recalled the explosion of processed and fast food brands of the 1950s, except "processed" and "fast" were now properties being repudiated, instead of embraced.[46]

The artisanal impulse proved to be boundless. It leapt from the world of food to the rest of American culture. The diffusion agents were sometimes obvious. Chefs who had finished their shifts would move to the restaurant bar for a drink and regale anyone who would listen about the Waters revolution. Before long, the bar was dominated by a new idea of ingredients and preparation. The bartender took on new craft and new dignity. There was a first florescence of the "mixol-ogy revolution" in 2001 and a second in 2006.[47] The artisanal move-ment would eventually jump to the American home, transforming domestic space and child-rearing there.

———

The biggest milestone in the Alice Waters revolution may have come in 2009, when Michelle Obama put a vegetable garden on the South Lawn of the White House. In a place where so many things are cere-monial and memorial, the then first lady's plot was a working "kitchen garden" designed for the practical purpose of supplying the White House table. When a trend transforms the White House, it has, in a real sense, arrived. The nation's reaction to the garden was almost as telling as the garden itself. The response was not, as it often is in our superheated political moment, "Oh my God, what does she think she's doing? That is hallowed ground!" No, the reaction from both Left and Right was more often, "Interesting. We're thinking about a vegetable garden of our own." Some things were bigger than politics. (And these days, it's astonishing to think there is anything bigger than politics.)

By this time, the artisanal impulse was no longer a slipstream phenomenon or even a merely upper-middle-class one. It had passed from fad to fashion to trend, and it was now on the verge of install-ing itself in American culture as a new set of preferences about food, food preparation, packaging, retail, the supply chain, the brand, nutri-tion, and even domestic life and child-rearing. You could see it in the grocery store, where the once triumphant center, filled with prepared and packaged goods, was shrinking. The outer boundary, filled with dairy and produce, was expanding. Consumer packaged goods were in free fall, and their executives were bailing out for new jobs in other economies. Alice Waters had won.

Thanks to Waters, consumers no longer admired big. They no longer admired industrial. Thanks to Alice Waters, they wanted something cozy, little, and charming. They cared less about status. They cared less about fashion. (Millennials actually cultivated something called "normcore," which was deliberately designed to be anti-status and anti-fashion.[48]) They cared less about competing with their neighbors. They were now about being kinder and gentler. This marked an almost complete repudiation of status-conscious America and its latest manifestation, the preppy movement. The polo shirt that once served as a badge of preppy membership now threatened to suggest that the wearer was a stuck-up, self-important loser.

## Okay, but What about Honor?

When Alice and her brain trust sat around the table at Chez Panisse, they were intent on transforming American life. The obvious target was all that processed, adulterated food, pumped full of sugar, fat, and salt, all the fast food that seemed designed to strip food of its nutrition, all, and especially, the things we fed our children: the breakfast cereal, the snacks, the desserts. Whatever else these were, they were sugar-delivery devices designed to turn children into industry shills. "Please, Mommy, may I have some more?"

Waters's telos was simple: change the way food is a farmed, harvested, transported, packaged, marketed, and taken to market, and you change family life. The rest of her revolution was less obvious and happened pretty much on its own. Change American food and family life, and a landslide is set in motion. Restaurants, retail, urban planning, marketing, storytelling would eventually follow suit. Did Alice Waters intend this immense act of social engineering? She hasn't said.

It seems unlikely that honor entered into her calculations. In the counterculture from which she came, the artisanal and mixology cultures she helped birth, honor was never mentioned at all. For the band of activists sitting around Waters's Chez Panisse table, it must have seemed that these grand acts of transformation must necessarily end in social good. After all, if Americans were eating better, in happier, less pretentious restaurants, in smaller, Jane Jacobs–scale neighborhoods, surely that could only have pleasant social effects. Surely, these Americans would be nicer to one another and better behaved. All of this was obvious and inevitable. In the 1970s, a reference to honor would surely have seemed old-fashioned and retrograde.

But the optimism of this movement is haunted by the ghost of the American historian Gertrude Himmelfarb, a woman with cultural ambitions of her own. Himmelfarb did not believe that the social reform unleashed in the twentieth century would necessarily result in a more moral world. Indeed, Himmelfarb wondered whether this carving away at the traditional order might lead to a demoralization. And it's hard to say she was wrong. Surely the bad behaviors of the present day do not spring from the artisanal revolution, or from any of the other cultural reforms of the twentieth century, but the social change we needed to accomplish them may have cost us some of our moral clarity.

Still, when we look at the Waters revolution it looks very much as if, intentionally or not, it prepared the way for the return of honor. Her revolution discouraged the fast food outlet, punched out with perfect uniformity across the country. It encouraged the rise of owner-operated places, run by young people who scorned the fast food model, who wanted their places, their food, their ambiance to be as individual and local as possible. The only uniformity sought in regard to coffeehouses was perfectly brewed coffee. (This left Starbucks struggling in the middle ground. It got the coffee mostly right, but would have to exert itself mightily not to look like a chain. And it would have to endure "baristas" who were deeply unhappy with the prospect of being mistaken for someone who answered to a central office.)

Unlike fast food places, coffee shops did not "process" consumers with industrial efficiency. They were not seen by consumers as places for sprinting through. McDonald's promised it would shave seconds off our visit. The local coffee shop was hoping we might linger, happy to keep us waiting as the barista got the foam pattern exactly right. Coffee shops were for coming back to day after day. The idea was that eventually you would get to know the owner and her staff. (I dare you to name the manager of your local McDonald's or Starbucks.) Eventually you would get to know other patrons. And before long local artists would be asking to put their work up. Then local poets would ask to stage a slam. This little café, when it works best, becomes a platform for the local community.

It took fully fifty years for the walk-to-town trend to visit my part of Connecticut.[49] But when it came, it turned lives and the real estate market upside down. People were now eager to sell the status trophy homes in Darien, the ones that sat on an acre or more, splendid in their isolation, self-adoring in their architecture. At some point in the past eight years, people began to think these places were kind of sad, embodying a pointless "distancing" (as we now call it) that appeared to estrange us from the social life we were beginning to think we cared about. Alice Waters had managed to touch even the lives of the 1 percent, people at the top of the social hierarchy, moving them to repudiate the things everyone was supposed to want and obliged to admire.

The walk-to-town trend was *designed* to take you to those little coffee shops. And it was designed to introduce you to your neighbors. Inevitably you would fall into step and into conversation. These were people you used to "wave to" as the phrase had it. Surely this was the true measure of American anomie, that the best you could hope for in grand neighborhoods were "waving rights." "Yeah, I know him. We wave to one other." It was almost as if Darien was enduring a COVID-19 outbreak well before the rest of us.

The walk-to-town trend made people visible in ways they had not been before. Showing up every day in coffee shops and other places, they were now located in social space. They were now *somewhere* instead of ceaselessly moving in the jet stream, swift selves in motion. People who slowed in social space existed over time. They could be judged. They could be found friendly, interested, useful, reliable . . . or not. They could be found honorable or not. Reputations could now be calculated. The reputation economy could be fired up. This was the advantage to intimate communities. Within certain limits, people knew who you were and would give you credit for some behavior and discredit for others. Wittingly or not, Americans had given up the Teflon that kept reputations from forming and communities from taking shape.

Smaller towns were likely to flourish with difference. Some would favor the arts, others commerce, still others education, nightlife, or fashion. They could all now create their own standards of judgment, their own honor economies. They were now in a position to turn once perfect strangers into moral beings who could accrue honor or shed it. Intentionally or not, Alice Waters helped accomplish even this.

## 4.6 The Treasure in Treasuring

Some months ago someone asked me to look at social life in the US. Some social scientists would approach this problem by crafting a fixed set of questions, attaching it to a clipboard, and firing up a group of investigators to collect data online or in person. But you use an anthropologist when you don't know *exactly* what you want to know.

The task is not to ask fixed questions. The task is to go fishing, to search out what respondents are thinking and feeling, and in this mass of rough answers to general questions detect an answer that takes us into the American experience.

A topic as broad as social life meant casting the net very widely indeed. I wanted to hear about the whole of people's lives, and when you give the respondent this much leeway, they are sure to end up going places you never expected, talking about things you never knew you wanted to know about.

So I was only mildly astonished when one of my respondents started telling me about what happens when she goes out with her friends to dinner. Charlotte (let's call her) said, "I just love being out with my friends." And she said it with such intensity that I was taken aback. She re-created the emotional tone of the event itself. She curled her arms up in front of her so that I could see the intimacy she was talking about. I could see how much she relished the moment, almost luxuriated in it. To be honest, I am not the most social person in the world, so I am often surprised by how much pleasure people find in social moments. But this I had never heard before. Charlotte was expressing a deeper, richer pleasure than I had seen before. She was *treasuring* her friends.

This might be new, especially when we think of all the ways Americans have contrived to find less pleasure in one another's company. Driven by the avant-garde impulse, people were so busy being cool, showing their detachment from the moment, this intensity of feeling was considered a little dopey. When status consumption was still active, treasuring was unfashionable, even gauche. (This is one of the things hipster poets and polite society have in common. They cultivate something one calls "cool," the other calls "sangfroid.") Swift selves made a bargain of their own. They said that every moment of social life was a way station on the path to the "next," as if the present were there to be repudiated so we could get on to the future. But Charlotte was luxuriating in her friends. She was being there now.

There are signs that this has been happening elsewhere in American culture. In 2011 Bob Greenblatt, then the head of NBC, took a look at the enormous success of *American Idol*, and while his competitors were desperate to build a lookalike, he created *The Voice*. The problem with *American Idol*, Greenblatt thought, was that Simon Cowell was the "dark judge," less a judge than a punisher. Greenblatt wanted a show that was supportive and positive. *The Voice* was that and then some. Contestants were not so much judged as coached. *The Voice* got 12 million viewers in its first season. On the strength of its success, Greenblatt began to focus on "unabashedly emotional shows." He commissioned *This Is Us*.[50] This registered 14 million viewers in the first season and 17.5 in the second.

Sentimentality. Maybe it's back. Once the marker of unsophisticated people, it is now okay, or at least okayer. Charlotte is, by all appearances, an entirely sophisticated person. There's no failure of taste and judgment here. There is never any sign of kitsch or corniness, nothing garish or overly personal. But here she was openly, quite happily, declaring the depth of her emotions.

What Charlotte was saying openly, others were admitting on the sly. An aperitif here is wine fortified with brandy and infused with flavor. It's a before-dinner drink, thought to stimulate the appetite. A return-to-aperitif trend broke out in New York City in 2014 and more broadly in 2018.[51] The trend was embraced by mixologists grateful to have a way to extend the mixology trend, but it was also embraced by boomers and millennials, each for their own reasons: it was low alcohol, which appealed to the first group, and nicely Instagrammable, which drew the second.

But the aperitif trend was, in the words of *Cleveland Scene* writer Ryan Irvine, a way to "slow things down." Irvine says, "The apéritif really is a statement of one's intentions. It implies: 'I'm here to eat, I'm here to enjoy myself and my company, and I'm in no hurry.'" It was a European import embraced by Americans to make themselves a little less American. In the words of Helena Price Hambrecht, cofounder of online wine merchant Haus, "apéritif culture has all of the qualities that today's generation of American drinkers want—it's more laid back, it's about people forming connections instead of partying hard. It's about drinking something complex and interesting versus drinking just to get drunk."[52]

Here it was again, but less obvious this time: Americans finding a way to spend more time with friends . . . for the sake of spending time with friends, for the sake of treasuring them. The aperitif helps shape exactly the event Charlotte treasures, especially when served at home. It helps you host an event with special friends in your most intimate space. Such entertaining is different from that done in a restaurant, where we once embraced the anonymity of the event, all of us serving as bit players amid the excitement and crowds that are hallmarks of a good restaurant. Now it's your friends, your place, your here, your now.

Treasuring represents a shift from an extrinsic view of life to an intrinsic one. It prizes our immediate circumstances, the people, the place, the event, the moment, for their own sake. These are not, as they used to be, way stations or stepping-stones.

This is a radical idea in the American context. And yes, to be sure, it has been practiced by some communities for some time. Those who meditate know it well. But for a mainstream American to speak as Charlotte does breaks faith with our once preferred temporal orientation and the old social order.

And this creates a context in which honor has hope. A world that has slowed enough that we can *see* one another more clearly and build reputations as we go. Honor needs the continuity of domestic life. Only thus are we known at all by our neighbors, our actions judged over time. Only thus can people decide who we are and whether we are honorable.

It's almost as if we are cultivating a plainness that makes each of us more visible. (Our Protestant forebears would be so pleased.) Now that we care less about conspicuous consumption, status mobility, and negotiating a world filled with strangers, now that we are living more simply, with less mobility, in small, more intimate communities, we are not just more visible. There are, in fact, fewer places to hide. The economist Tibor Scitovsky argued that there was a dark side to our ceaseless movement. It made us take things for granted. But in the forty-five years since he wrote this, we have stepped away from a mobile world to one that's much stiller. And whether we intend this or not, this is a world honor likes.[53]

# 4.7 Most Millennials Are Lying to You

Here's another dispatch from the anthropologist's notebook. Pretty recent, too. I was on a project, studying young people, once more trying to get a picture of their social lives.

I found myself talking to millennials and Gen Zers (henceforth "millennials" for both). These people were talking about office parties. It was that time of the year.

"What happens?" I asked. The answers were various and interesting, but eventually it became clear there was one "truth" circulating in the data that none of my respondents were prepared to come right out and tell me.

Specifically: that these millennials were faking it. They were behaving at these parties in a manner that was a little disingenuous. They were *pretending* to be boomers, concealing the millennial within!

"Hey," I said finally, "it sounds like you're faking it!" (Sometimes you just name the elephant.)

"Well, yeah."

"Really?"

"It's what you have to do sometimes."

Some millennials see some boomers as creatures from another culture, as people with their own language, values, rituals, and preoccupations. And they have come to realize that cross-cultural communication is only possible if the millennial handles the boomer with the utmost care. The millennial must reassure the boomer that she knows and accepts boomer world. Only then can things go smoothly.

This strategy leads some boomers to believe that their point of view is everyone's point of view. And it forces millennials, in a sense, underground, causing them to conceal their *own* language, values, rituals, and preoccupations. How grim. One generation is duped, the other denied. But boomers are worse than duped. They are also patronized. People tiptoe around them, so as not to "startle the horses." And millennials are worse than denied. They are also effaced.

This piece of generational cunning is unusual in American youth culture. Most youth cultures come out swinging. They mock and scorn previous generations. They protest their difference and insist upon it. God knows boomers did this. They openly ridiculed their parents. But millennials took a more surreptitious approach to things. They have lived as spies among us. There wasn't anything deep about their cover—there didn't have to be. Boomers were so persuaded of the sufficiency of their world, it never occurred to them that anyone around them wasn't entirely on board.

The depth and success of the millennial deception changed recently. Suddenly, the phrase "OK boomer" emerged. (I'll put the launch date here as around November 2019.[54]) A flare went up in the darkness. Apparently, not all millennials were prepared to indulge their elders. They began to signal their impatience. Out loud. In public. And damn the consequences.

But this is, by the looks of things, an early indicator. For the moment, and for at least the short term, millennials and Gen Zers continue to live under deep cover, to fake a compliance with boomers they do not feel.

I can't give an explanation. I have yet to do the ethnographic work that would allow me to see what brought millennials to this strategy and why they insist on it. But I can speculate. And I will.

———

I believe one point of contention is "culture."

Boomers have been reluctant to embrace this idea. Indeed, they have mostly excluded it from conversation and from business. On planet Boomer, culture tends to be synonymous with entertainment, and light entertainment at that—specifically Hollywood movies and TV shows with a measure of youthful innovation too small and too marginal to count for much. What comes from Hollywood and TV is not really culture. It is not something to be taken seriously or to be talked about, studied, or embraced with passion. It is after all, merely entertainment, merely noise.

And here's the kicker. The moment a boomer realizes that popular culture would reward more careful study is the moment they realize they must now devote a couple of years to bringing themselves up to speed. This will mean concerted study of music, TV, movies, YouTube videos, graffiti, music, contemporary fiction, anime, and, yes, album art. Confronted with this catching up, it is easier to say, "You know what, entertainment is just fluff. It doesn't really mean anything. I'm good." And this is a perfectly sensible thing to say . . . at least as long as we don't impose it on everyone else. The boomer is surrounded by younger generations that know and love this culture. Look to them.

Grimes's music has the same quality as her album art. Chris Will calls it a "radio transmission from a dance club in a distant galaxy," one that manages to combine both the ethereal and the subterranean to an effect that is sometimes lithe, sometimes violent.[55] This multiplicity has consequences. Grimes says, "Most of my music is unplaylistable. Which is a huge problem: 'This is not pop. This is not rock.' They're not discernible genres."[56]

Genre. Many boomers live by genre. Their music comes in genre boxes. Rock, rhythm and blues, jazz, dance, electronic. Genre was how radio stations—which were the way boomers were introduced to music in their youth—knew what to play. A melodic lockstep. It was music formed by genre, and then repeated endlessly. Pop radio is pap radio. Or so it sounds, if you've been listening to the music from a distant galaxy.

Meanwhile, the music outside of the well-worn genres of past decades is changing furiously. Take the case of live music, and especially the music festival. The festival has all the animation and the imperfections of the live performance and it takes place in a small village, filled with people doing many things as they listen. They wander. They buy stuff. They have lunch. They snuggle. They write poetry.

(The scene recalls historian Keith Thomas's description of what Eliza-bethans did while sitting through very long services. Yes, they listened. They also knitted, ate, read, and, in some cases, let off guns.[57])

What does this mean? Music leapt off the recording, out of the radio, into a muddy field filled with people getting wicked sunburns. And this performance became, for many fans, the definitive version of the music in question. Live music trumps even the studio-enabled perfections of the recorded version. As scholar Henry Jenkins has told us, what used to be derivative is now definitional.[58] Try getting a boomer into any field to listen to music these days. Try. For boomers, a live performance is the imperfect reproduction of the original. Now they are what defines it.

But it's not just music that has slipped the bonds of genre. Self-hood has, too. For boomers, theirs were standard-issue selfhoods, ap-proved by the middle class and the mainstream. These were, as we have seen, broadened by hippies, made cooler by the avant-garde, sharp-ened by the swift-self regime, and brought to performance readiness by a celebrity culture. Boomers were touched by all these social in-novations. But generally speaking, they do not look to popular culture for the "raw feed" of innovation with which to continue their per-sonal expansion. Generally speaking, they are done, fixed in place. Not for them the transformational enthusiasms of Gen Y and Gen Z. The latter take for granted that they will continue to work with materials supplied to them by popular culture.

Here it is in a nutshell. For younger generations, Grimes is a crea-tive force who might come up with something that helps define who you are and the world as you wish to see it. For older generations, she's engaged in an outlandish act of eccentricity. She's not making culture, she's making noise.

The greatest generational divide is over hip-hop. Older listeners tend to become instantly censorious. There is something wrong, something monstrous about this music. Surely it celebrates illegality. What if it *provokes* illegality? This is boomer gospel. But if you are younger, hip-hop is the soundtrack of your life. It is filled with the diverse astonishments created by Lil Wayne, Jay-Z, Kanye West, Chance the Rapper. It's a laboratory for the creation of sense and sensibility. All these parties, from Grimes to Chance the Rapper, are world and identity builders.

These two very different ideas of popular culture would not matter so much except that boomers and millennials do occasionally find themselves trying to solve the same problem, then find themselves at loggerheads. This is especially true when it comes to running an organization. Boomers are fond of thinking that culture doesn't matter very much when it comes to business. Culture is additional. It's superficial, in every sense of the word. It's something we slap on, something we can therefore strip away. And that, boomers think, is the job of smart, tough-minded people. Boomers take pride in removing anything that doesn't speak to the practical, the utilitarian, the consumer's pursuit of economic self-interest.

And this is why they must then "go ask the intern." Having removed culture, they must now find a way to add it back in. They reach a certain point in some set of deliberations and think, *Hm, I wonder if this makes any sense to the world out there. Someone go find the intern.* Millennials sitting at the table sometimes think to themselves, *Well, you could have asked me.* They might even be thinking, *You might actually have bothered to learn enough about contemporary culture that you could answer that question yourself.* The most likely answer is "OK boomer."

I know some of this from my research for Netflix. They asked me to look at how people were watching TV now that it streamed in entire seasons at the viewer's choice of time and place. It turned out that the Netflix effect was profiting from a revolution that had been in the works for more than a decade. TV had been getting better. Virtuous cycles were drawing in better writers, actors, directors, producers. Each gave courage and license to the last. And together they created smarter viewers and all the cycles began again. By the year 2000, if you wanted to make TV, you had to speak to your viewers as much as you "entertained" them.

But some boomers continue to act as if TV were a boob tube. They committed heavily to the idea that TV was a "wasteland." And now they can't let go. Thus many of them are condemned to hours of *Law & Order* episodes. How do I know? My career sometimes takes me into a close orbit around the academic world, and this means that, come Friday afternoon, I join my colleagues in the common room for drinks and collegial chatter. The moment the TV topic comes up, they begin to recite the intellectual's rosary. "Oh, we don't have a TV." Or, "Well, we have a TV but we only watch PBS." Or . . . it goes on and on. These academics are desperate to let you know that they are serious, nay, weighty intellectuals. So of course they scorn TV. It's for children and simpletons.

I can suffer fools gladly. I really can. Because I know, eventually, that when the sherry hits the bloodstream, these people will begin to strike up positively Talmudic conversations about particular *Law & Order* episodes. Because of course they watch TV. Everyone watches TV.

All popular culture got better. In fact, as the Canadian writer Hargurchet Bhabra once put it, it's time to drop the adjective. It's not popular culture. It's just culture. And all of this happened under boomers' noses. And this makes them look odd to millennials—like eighteenth-century monarchs who insist on rituals of courtesy and shows of power even as the rest of the world has moved on to new philosophies and theater.

## How Does Honor Fit Here?

Millennials are not wrong to dissemble, to pretend their boomer-planet compliance, to fake it. If there is one truth that has revealed itself to anthropology, it is that social life depends upon small deceptions. This begins with white lies like, "No, I love this dish." If we did not occasionally lie, we would be intolerable to one another. If we did not sometimes fake it, we would be in a state of constant antagonism. Would it help if millennials told us the grim truth about ourselves? (I speak now as a boomer.) It might. On the other hand, life is easier for everyone if we all go along for the sake of appearances.

But there are real costs to millennial deception. Boomers are surrounded by people who are not what they seem. And this makes them a little like aging Hollywood stars, living in a bubble inflated by people's esteem and eventually withering under their contempt. In a culture filled with constant innovation and new species of social life, boomers are obliged to assume that their worldview is not the only one.

Contemporary culture produces a super-fluid social life, and to scorn it would be unwise. After all, scorn is the reflex of old honor systems. It reflects the insider's privilege. Elizabethans took for granted that they were defined and confined by the social world. Victorians chafed a bit more, but they, too, bowed before convention. Diminishment and scorn were the tools used to uphold these honor systems and to police privilege.

Our honor system needs to be more porous, more responsive. Our honor must honor others. We can't give honor unless we know what honor is. This means that there is no dismissing of others. There can be no willful ignorance. We can't pretend that we are creatures of privilege, the ones who set the tone and call the shots. We should want to see the genius of Grimes, or, if we can't, to defer to those who do.

The new honor gives no right of judgment. No insider's advantage. There are no insiders. There are only strangers in our midst. We can ignore them, but surely that's a bad idea. Because it is always better to know than not to know. We are richer for it. And insisting that we may judge is the surest way to make ourselves look like Macy's parade floats: big, dumb dirigibles floating well above the realities of contemporary life.

But there is one place this honor code will not go. It does not know or care about the particulars of identity. It accepts that escaping the tyranny of fixed and forced identities was one of the great accomplishments of the twentieth century, that we were now increasingly free to make our own choices, craft our own personhood.

The new honor code doesn't take a position on identity. In the language of Elizabeth I, identities are a "thing indifferent," something we do not specify or presume to issue. This honor system says identity is a matter of personal choice and that people will exercise this right as they see fit. Honor doesn't presume to know better. It has forsaken its right to sort or form the social world. It merely wants to assess what we have done for others, what social good we have created. Whoever else we are doesn't matter. Honor is not about "who"; it's about "what"—what we have done for others.

## 4.8 Summing Up

The twentieth century was a cauldron of invention. We reimagined ourselves over and over again. We have reviewed a few of our reinventions here: the avant-garde, celebrity celebrants, swift creatures, hippies, artisans, and a couple of new shapes that belong more to the twenty-first century than the twentieth century.

None of this invention appears to have cared about honor at all. Fundamental changes to the social life of the Anglo-American world, sweeping changes to selfhood, family life, community, and capitalism—all this reimagining was done without wondering whether the idea that had so organized the Western tradition would come in handy. Well, you might say, the idea had slipped into obscurity. But that's not true. Honor was there in all the novels we still read from the nineteenth century. It was visible to anyone who was a student of the liberal arts. It was there in the literature of heroism. It was the very language with which we memorialized the sacrifices made by people in World Wars I and II. No one who has ever looked at a war memorial can have escaped the term. Honor was there for anyone who had committed to military life and to us all as consumers of the abundant novels and movies that celebrate military heroism.

Indeed, the social movements we have looked at here could almost be seen to seek the tearing-down of honor.

The avant-garde found honor stuffy on the one hand and slavish on the other. Honor was a bourgeois value. It was the kind of thing only polite society cared about. It represented the values of a bourgeois society. Honor was a lie, a deception, something we had been tricked into caring about. Historically, honor meant the end of selfhood. To commit to it meant removing ourselves from the Romantic search for personal and social truths. As Jack Kerouac might have said, honor was for idiots—not the glamorous losers celebrated by Leonard Cohen in one generation and by Beck in a later one, but the people who couldn't see that their loyalty to social convention destroyed all hope of getting to the truth.

Celebrities matter for their beauty and their talent. They would also have us admire them for their causes. (And we do. Except, of course, when the star in question is Jessica Biel or Jenny McCarthy and the cause is anti-vaccination.) We admire them as cultural pioneers. But we cannot look away from this: celebrities are in it for celebrities. They engage in a self-aggrandizement that does not appear to leave much room for honor. They are no friend of honor.

Swift selves were appealing in their way. There wasn't much posturing. Everyone was pretty frank about their mission. For all their status aspirations, swift selves didn't know from honor. They were too busy making their way in the world. As we have seen, the treasuring movement has helped end the reign of the swift self. People are settling in time and place. This is very good for honor. But the swift regime had made a contribution of its own. It completed the world of individualism and made a new honor possible out of the ruins of the old.

Hippies scorned the suburbs, hoping for the attainment of novel spiritualities, socialities, consciousnesses. Mission largely accomplished. Artisans went to work on another piece of American convention. They took on the food industry and enemies like Applebee's, a fast food chain that was owned by a company called DineEquity, its name an inedible neologism that captured capitalism's hostility toward food. Over and over again, social innovations rose up to transform the American experience. And in none of these moments did it occur to anyone that the restoration of honor might be a good idea.

All of the social innovations named so far have done two things. They've driven our culture away from honor. But they've also succeeded in preparing us for its return.

# CHAPTER 5

## Honor's Refuge

We live in what author James Bowman calls a "post honor culture."[1] Somewhere between the Elizabethan period and the present day, honor fell away. In the previous section, we looked at some of the things that laid it low. These include the birth of the avant-garde, the dawn of a celebrity culture, the rise of American modernism, and that great wave of dishonorable behavior that has ensued in public life.

Honor has been made to look clueless, old-fashioned, and out of touch. It has even been accused of being the villain of the piece. As Adam Kirsch suggests in *The Atlantic,*

> most of the moral advances of modern society—from the abolition of slavery to the emancipation of women—start to look like victories over an antiquated ideal of honor.[2]

To make matters still worse, honor has been libeled as the driving force behind violent and lawless crime families (see, for example, Mafia movies by Martin Scorsese and Francis Ford Coppola.)

For all this, honor was scorned and disparaged. It was viewed as a remnant of a world we were lucky to have seen the last of. Any remaining trace of honor was called an atavistic survival, the past living on autonomically in the nervous system of the body politic. Honor was over. Many people said good riddance.

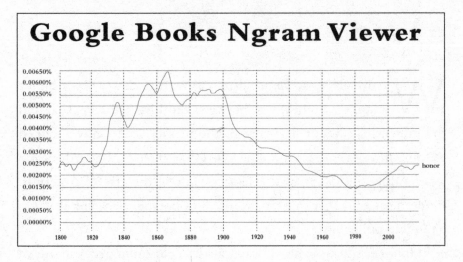

# Google Books Ngram Viewer

The decline of honor was long. If we look at Google's Ngram (a system for showing how often a term appears on the published page), we see "honor" decline starting around 1860. Things really get bad around 1900, when honor goes into free fall; it bottoms out around 1980, and has since made a modest recovery. There's a small uptick after 2000, possibly owing to 9/11.

In all of this, there was one refuge for honor. One institution offered it protection. One community took honor in. Some groups made it the cardinal objective of daily life. These were the military and the first responders who use the military as their model.

The military kept faith even when doing so gave others license to dishonor them. Soldiers returning from service in Vietnam were spat upon and showered with abuse. (This is a special test, when embracing honor is used against you.)

It was clear that if I really wanted to know about modern honor, I was going to have to talk to some soldiers and first responders. But doing so would not be easy. Most Americans can call up someone they know in the military and say, "Hey, can we talk about honor, please? What's the 411 there?" But I was born and raised in Canada, where the military is much smaller. (In fact, Canada's military is not much larger than that of Thailand.) To a boy growing up in Vancouver on the country's west coast, it was almost invisible. I didn't know anyone.

For an anthropologist, this is really, really bad. This is data free fall. I didn't know what to think, or where to start.

Then I remembered that some of my students at the Harvard Business School were ex-military. One of them distinguished himself in the classroom one morning by performing the single most acrobatic piece of problem-solving I'd ever seen at Harvard, in the classroom or the faculty lounge. It was as though he performed a kind of double backflip from the prone position, sticking a perfect landing. The class was stunned into silence. They could see what had just happened. We were only a few minutes into the class, and the case was cracked. The class was over. Finally one student said, "Good night, everyone. Drive safely!"

I had a couple of illuminating conversations here and there, but I didn't feel I was getting to the root of things. That's the thing about military honor: it is deeply embedded in the organization. And like any value that's deeply embedded, it's hard to bring to the surface.

I needed to see honor more plainly. I remembered reading about flags in a book by Rich Lowry called *The Case for Nationalism*. Lowry says flags figured so greatly in the Civil War that some Northerners called it the "War Against the Flag." Lowry continues,

> Color sergeants risked life and limb carrying the flag in the battle and keeping it flying and out of enemy hands. Seven corporals of the 99th Pennsylvania Volunteer Infantry died protecting the flag at Gettysburg, right around the spot where Lincoln gave his address. At the Battle of Fredericksburg, one sergeant in the 5th New Hampshire Volunteer was wounded and handed it over to yet another sergeant, who took the flag to a mortally wounded captain so he could die with it in his arms.[3]

You might think, *If a flag is so important, soldiers would have kept it safe at camp.* But these soldiers took it into battle. They put it in harm's way. They exposed it to capture. And that helps us see not just that a flag mattered but how. A solider wanted to enter battle under a streaming flag because it expressed will. It summoned courage. It struck terror.

The color sergeant carrying the flag into battle made himself a target. The enemy wanted to bring him and the flag low. A marksman could see exactly where he was. The flag tracked him as he moved.

To carry the flag was an act of courage. In the Gettysburg case, men died carrying the flag, and a succession of men took it up with the knowledge that it might mean their deaths, too.

We could say this was honor's contract. A soldier picked up the flag because he or she knew predecessors had taken it up before and a line of successors would take it up after. This was a kind of generational contract. It made a fighting force something larger than, and encompassing of, the lives of individual soldiers.

It was also a kind of contract with the enemy. Terms are spelled out. As with all good contracts, assurances are given. Outcomes are promised. This flag is ours. This is us. The flag is—we are—triumphant. The flag is—we are—formidable. The flag is—we are—unbeatable. You will not take our flag.

And one soldier at the Battle of Fredericksburg believed, in the press of battle, that his comrade should die embracing the flag. Was this because the dying man was returning to the embrace of his company and his cause? To die with honor is to achieve immortality.

I am no expert, obviously, but it seems as though a flag is a material representation of the things honor stands for—the who, what, and why of sacrifice. Flags are (perhaps) honor made manifest.

These days, we make honor manifest in different ways. I came across a book by Senator Tom Cotton of Arkansas. Cotton was a platoon leader in the "Old Guard," the Third United States Infantry. He served at Arlington National Cemetery between his tours of combat in Iraq and Afghanistan. His book is called *Sacred Duty: A Soldier's Tour at Arlington National Cemetery.*

This book offers, among other things, a detailed account of how the Old Guard honors the dead. Their work is defined by perfect execution. Every detail of dress, comportment, and ceremony must be specified exactly and rendered faultlessly. For instance, a soldier in the Old Guard, having started the installation of flags, "must finish any row he starts, because different boot sizes might disrupt the perfect symmetry of the headstones and flags."[4]

Senator Cotton says the task given the OG is to "embody the meaning of words such as patriotism, duty, honor, and respect. These soldiers are the most prominent public face of our Army, perform the sacred last rites for our fallen heroes, and watch over them into eternity." The demands of ritual and ceremony are grueling. Soldiers stand at attention for hours in heavy wool uniforms sometimes soaked in sweat. Some, a very few, keel over. They are replaced immediately. The imperfection is erased.[5]

Some of this ceremonial work is performed for families who come to honor a relative interred at Arlington. But some of the work is performed for the OG itself.

Just as we posted the colors in the morning, we retired the colors after the last full-honor funeral. The ceremony was a simple salute from the troops to the flag. Again, we could have skipped it; no one would see, by design. But we went the extra distance to honor the flag—the flag worn by the soldiers we buried that day, the flag that adorned their remains, the flag that their loved ones now carried back to their home.[6]

Senator Cotton observes the several things Arlington honor accomplishes. Honor is remembrance. It's a way to deal with tragedy, pain, and loss. It's a reply to sacrifice. It memorializes the contracts those Civil War flags helped create and fulfill.

Reading *Sacred Duty*, you begin to see why the work of the OG has to be perfect. The point of the ritual is honor, and honor isn't achieved unless the ritual is perfect. Only by exerting ourselves fully and perfectly can we adequately honor the dead.

There it is again. I just said something close to "It is only by honoring the dead that the OG can honor the dead." That's the thing about military honor. It is constantly looping back on itself. It does this both as a contract and as a weaving of cause and effect. Honor inspires honor, which requires honor, which provokes honor. It's a rich and layered idea. It keeps folding over on itself. Yes, exactly. Like a flag.

I also found an essay by Sandra Gibson,[7] a member of ATEC, the US Army Test and Evaluation Command. She was charged with describing honor. And she does it elegantly in a couple hundred words.

Gibson says honor is a value that stands for all the other military values (respect, duty, loyalty, self-service, integrity, and personal service). Honor is summoned in us by the flag, the anthem, the heroism of others. It is an emotion, rising, stirring, and moving us to honorable behavior. It begets honor in us. And this behavior begets honor in others. Honor creates honor, and that honor then inspires honor. Cause and effect weave together again.

Honor is integral to the causes and the effects of military life itself. It's where things start and where they end, and how they work in between. And this, in a way I had not fully appreciated, helps explain the true horror of the way soldiers were treated in American airports during the Vietnam War. These airports, where men were spat upon for upholding their values, the honor they believed in, were the complete opposite of Arlington. Their experiences there must have made some soldiers wonder if the country for which they fought deserved their service. Honor's contract was violated. That these soldiers managed to persevere in service tells you that the idea of honor has extraordinary powers of persistence. Of all the work it does, this is perhaps the most remarkable. It can sustain itself even when dishonored. It is indestructible.

You can see that I am struggling to give an account of military honor. I am out of my depth and working with insufficient data and experience. And, believe me, I understand that there is something loathsome about writing clumsily about an idea for which people have sacrificed their lives. I get that and I apologize. That is the only honorable thing to do. But I hope I have said enough to suggest that honor lives on in the American experiment and that it is every bit as robust and definitional in military life as anything we saw in the Elizabethan period. I think it's probably true to say there is little chance we could make the idea of military honor live "on the outside," in civilian life. But perhaps we can honor it by trying.

## CHAPTER 6

# Rebuilding Honor

This chapter is designed to set up the one to follow, chapter 7, and our honor code. Think of it as the lab bench, a place to work out problems and concepts. The final code will be small and compressed. It will require a great many assumptions. This is the place to puzzle some of those out. (You never get all of them.)

## Adding On

The honor code is designed to sit on top of other moral systems that guide our lives. There's no point in reinventing the wheel, or repudiating what has gone before. And you can't ask people to walk away from their existing commitments. This honor must work as an add-on, not a replacement.

There will be some points of conflict, places were the honor code *does* contradict moral precedent. For instance, Christianity counsels humility. I'm sorry, but honor doesn't do humility. It would like to, but it just can't. But this is a smallish difference, and not, I hope, a deal breaker in the theological scheme of things.

The new honor code can be an add-on for some purposes, but not all. It must learn to live with the various currents and crosscurrents in our culture. For those who still sustain a countercultural sensibility, honor is a dangerous thing. It distracts us from celestial harmonies, human goodness, and the reformation of private and public life. Indeed, as we labored to show in chapter 4, *most* of the social and cultural innovations of the twentieth century were indifferent or hostile to honor. American culture was busy charting new cultural territories and new models of the self. Honor seemed inherently allied to the old cultural territories and models of the self. By design or simple accident, we moved steadily away from the honor option.

So there are the moral problem and the social problem, but both come down to the same thing. We can't ask people to repudiate their moral commitments. And we can't ask them to repudiate the cultural and social innovations of the twentieth century. That's why we want to treat the honor code as a "thing indifferent," as Elizabeth I might have called it. Honor doesn't presume to transform moral life or cultural identity. It says, "Craft our lifestyle as we want. Define the self that works for us." But honor honor, too. So we can be club denizens, bikers, craft enthusiasts, long-distance runners, survivalists, downtown artists or/and uptown snobs. It shouldn't matter. Honor does not presume to make overarching demands on who we are or how we live. It merely says, "Render this one thing unto Caesar; all the rest is up to you."

That was, in a sense, my test with this book. Could Ken, Drew, Erin, Bob, and Jim all use the honor code? Would it work for all of them, despite their differences?

## Politics and Honor

Here's a problem I think I failed to solve: making honor equally useful across the political spectrum. Technically, it should serve us all, whatever our ideological inclinations. But in practice, it is often seen to be the friend of the Right and the enemy of the Left. This is a historical legacy, and chances are it will defeat my effort to resurrect an honor code across the board.

Here's why. I have political convictions, but I never lead with them. My job as an anthropologist is to figure out your politics, not to broadcast my own. (I figure one less combatant on the political battlefield will not matter in the larger scheme of things.) My job, in other words, is to act less like an American (or even a Canadian) and more like a Martian.

Here's what a Martian sees: at root, American political differences fall into two camps. Let's call these "Landscape" and "Portrait." (Hey, I'm a Martian. Expect weird metaphors! Martians found this distinction in a Microsoft Word manual and they are obsessed with it. We don't know why.)

How does this apply to politics? Here's how a Martian sees it. Some Americans are Portrait people. When presenting themselves in public, they put their best face forward. This means discovering and fulfilling the roles assigned them. Members of this group want to stand up and be counted. But this is not just a public image. It is also the way they see themselves. They believe what matters about them is their ability to fulfill responsibilities to the world, to family, community, and the state.

Other Americans prefer to "go landscape." They wish to present themselves not in a prescribed role, but closer to the way they "really" are. They adopt facial expressions and body postures that are more naturalistic. A little spontaneity helps to suggest their private selves or at least their individuality. In a sense, we see "into" them. The Landscape crew wants to embody the very things Portraitists seek to remove: individuality, creativity, distinctness. No stuffing themselves into public roles. No standard-issue selfhood.

Neither of these groups likes the other. The Portrait gang finds the Landscape gang self-indulgent. Individuality? Just do your job! Personality? Oh, please. Make an effort! Personality, that's for personal time. When presenting ourselves in public to strangers, it's not about the personal.

The loathing is reciprocated. The Landscape gang says the Portrait gang looks phony, artificial, and inauthentic. Indeed, the Portrait gang can sometimes seem to be withholding information, perhaps deliberately. These people, the Landscape gang say, cannot be trusted.

Different values point the two groups in entirely different directions. ("Humans!" as Martians like to shrug.) And this affects the way they think about honor. The Portrait gang see it as roughly correct.

The Landscape gang see it as an authoritarian abomination, an attack on their freedoms.

I have tried to depoliticize honor, to make it work for both Landscape and Portrait. I have sought to engineer an escape from these ideological differences. In point of fact, this honor code doesn't care about your politics. Again, it says, "Give this small thing to Caesar. The rest belongs to you." Will this protect me from the skepticism of the Landscape crew? I would be very surprised if it does. But alas, we must move on.

## Honor Is Small but Tough

The honor code needs to be a small set of instructions, just a few rules. Ten of them, actually. A nice round number. I want to keep the injunctions as simple of possible, make them easier to learn, easier to remember. We have not yet issued a laminated card for wallet or purse, but this could change.

And we want the code to be realistic. It is not merely a call to our nobler inclination. It accepts that humans are only sometimes virtuous, and more often self-interested and even monstrous. For the TV executive who installs a lock on the door of his office, no call to his essential goodness will discourage this behavior—or protect his colleagues. The honor code is designed to give him something to lose: in this case, his celebrity, power, and income.

In this sense, the honor code is unforgiving and unrelenting. It wants to specify the right thing to do and then insist it be done. Forget the imploring, the pleading, the appeals to goodness. Honor is impatient and suspicious. It says, "I have told you what to do. Now get on with it."

Honor is a little obnoxious. It doesn't want to inspire us. In the serious business of good behavior, inspiration is misplaced. It's good for certain spiritual purposes, to be sure—for raising our sights, lifting our aspirations. But to create good behavior in the social world, we need something more pragmatic. These are matters too important to be left to our better angels. (I say this as someone who spent most of his life in the twentieth century, as you probably did, where better angels failed spectacularly to protect good humans from bad ones.)

## Obnoxious, Even

To be honest, honor is a self-important jerk. Not always nice to have around, sort of like that bumptious friend from college we tolerate because he has a heart of gold and proves really useful on moving day.

We are unlikely to *like* honor. And it honestly doesn't care. It says, "I am vastly better than a Harvard soccer team that diminishes your daughter or a Wells Fargo that issues fake credit cards in your name. So deal with it."

There is *one* sense in which honor is cooperative and collaborative. It seeks to build something like a social enterprise. It's crowd-sourced. It won't work at all unless we sign up lots of people. And then those people will have to work together. They will have to agree on what is honorable, who is honorable, and how to honor those who are and dishonor those who are not. This is the only way to build an "honor economy."

But even here, honor is coercive. The honor economy may well *seem* voluntary. Honor wants you to know it is not. So make that "co-operative, collaborative, but obligatory."

This will provoke the suspicion that honor is a friend to authoritarianism, that it is oppressive, seeking conformity in thought and feeling and hierarchical command and control. (I think this is why some people think it's natural that the military took honor in. Why they see the military this way is another question entirely.)

Quite, quite wrong. The honor code has no interest in our heads or our hearts. It merely says, "Follow these few rules. If we get the honor economy up and running, we can unlock the reservoirs of good behavior that stand ready to flood the body politic like a generous spring runoff." And that would be good.

## External Honor

There are two kinds of honor: one external, one internal. External honor works like an economy. People seek benefit and value, and they work hard to protect themselves from loss. Bob, the guy we talked about in chapter 2, lives in an honor economy. Kinda. In fact, as we have seen, he has been close to heroic in his efforts to improve his community. What's weird is that he is not really the beneficiary of these efforts. People don't see Bob in the street and say, "Oh, that's the guy who . . ." Apparently, they take Bob's best efforts for granted, refusing him even so much as a "Thank you very much."

An honor economy would reward Bob—not because it loves Bob, but because it loves his community. Bob is good for the rest of us, so we want more Bobs. And we won't get more Bobs until we stop being stingy with our praise. Let's stop being stingy with our praise.

There is a cultural rule that gets in the way here. It says that people should be modest, that they should not claim credit. It's a very popular rule. We see it played out over and over again. A firefighter risks life and limb to save a family from a burning building. The six o'clock news shows up with praise and the reply is, "I'm just happy they're okay. But listen, I'm no hero. I was just doing my job. Any firefighter would have done the same."

Oh, for crying out loud. This has to stop. In an honor economy, the news anchor would say, "Are kidding me? You're an absolute hero. [*Looks into camera.*] Where's the parade, people? How about a statue for this guy? Am I right?" Of course, we're never going to get the firefighter to change. Humility is baked deep into the culture of the firehouse. But the rest of us, beginning with the news anchor, have to begin to make an effort to celebrate these people.

Let's be honest. As it stands, we're asking our heroes to work for scale. And in Bob's case, we're asking him to work for free. Economies must course with value. They have to distribute something. And that something begins with us. It begins with praise.

Our stinginess with accolades is very strange, because, as near as I can figure, admiration is free. It costs us nothing to sing the praises of Bob or a firefighter. Nothing.

Or maybe it does. A shadow of anthropological suspicion crosses our path. There might be a stinginess contained in our individualism. Maybe, in some way, we see admiration as a zero-sum game. What we give, we lose. The esteem I give to you comes out of the esteem I have for myself. Could this be? Is this possible? Are we so small that we would withhold our thanks to someone who has just stepped into the mouth of an inferno or spent his life building Little League diamonds and old folks' homes?

What, in short, is wrong with us? Let's rework the calculus. Surely, lavishing praise on others, even if it does cost us a little self-esteem, is a good bargain. Surely, withholding praise is just dumb . . . and petty . . . and becomes us not at all. In fact, it's dishonorable.

There is a second cultural rule that matters here. This one says, "Good deeds are their own reward." I have talked to Bob. We walk Grey and chat about stuff. This is exactly what he says: "I want to give back." And I think to myself, speaking now on behalf of honor, *Oh, snap out of it. It works for you, that's obvious. But most of the world wants to get paid. And your modesty, Bob, is not above? You should be demanding more. And when you don't, we're all poorer.*

This much is clear: if one Bob is good, ten Bobs are better. What if we could get ten people to do good things for the community? As long as we're not paying them, they are inclined to stay home and mow the lawn. If we want good works, we are going to have to pay for them.

Let's go back to the paradox from chapter 2, the one that says that sometimes people are prepared to admire *some* people and to pay them in admiration. Recall the praise for Ken the cheesemonger. He is lauded. Ken is the "Big Cheese." He runs a fabulous store. And of course, I know from my own experience that Ken is a prince of a guy. But why does he get this praise when people like Bob get none? How does he escape our zero-sum stinginess?

The same is true for Drew, our town storyteller, the creator of a writing school (and someone who, in the COVID-19 era, reads bedtime stories to kids on Zoom). People adore Drew. I know this because, again, when I am walking with her, she is always getting little waves from passersby and especially drivers-by, ones that say, "You are *so* dear to me." (And yes, as a trained anthropologist, I can tell what little waves mean.)

What, in short, is the difference between Bob, Jim, and Erin on the one side, and Ken and Drew on the other? Part of it is that Bob, Jim, and Erin are doing workaday work. It's not glamorous or fashionable. They are building Little League diamonds and creating safe highways by handing out tickets, whereas Drew is turning a writing class into a vehicle of self-exploration and self-expression for her students. And Ken is helping to liberate people in Darien from their status theater and helping them build social occasions that are rich and interesting.

Ewww! Is that it? Are we prepared to reward some people in the honor economy only if they are a) doing something fashionable, and/ or b) doing something that quite directly benefits the praise-giver? Or, to put this more precisely, is it a fact that we only surrender praise when there is something in it for us? How sad. Bob is making older people comfortable. Jim is making highways safe, but really, who cares?

It's all so very shortsighted, isn't it? Yes, we get something special from Ken and Drew. But in a way, we get something even more precious from Bob, Jim, and Erin. This is what cultural anthropologist Marshall Sahlins would call generalized exchange.[1] When we give praise to Bob, Jim, and Erin, we create more Bobs, Jims, and Erins, and these people create still more social value, and this eventually returns to us in the form of a better town. An honor economy will, in a vulgar phrase, "pay for itself." In fact, the "return on investment" is pretty spectacular.

It's also unbelievably selfish to withhold praise. There is an eighty-year-old who lives in quiet, calm, warmth, and dignity because Bob made an effort. The rest of us? Apparently we couldn't care less. Without Bob, this eighty-year-old faces a rooming house occupied by predators, but hey, that's okay. We're okay. And that's the important thing.

Part of the problem might also be that we're afraid of creating monsters. Do we fear that if we start handing out praise, we will end up living with egotists and divas and people who like to strut about demanding the admiration we would prefer to give voluntarily? This is not an unrealistic fear. I remember a public event at Harvard where a man of real standing in the academic community, clearly a brilliant guy, stood on the edge of the audience and kept strutting back and forth giving us dramatic looks as if to say, "Behold, I am here, I walk among you, I am magnificent." It reminded me of the criticism rendered by a sixteenth-century observer against young men who, he said, tried "to rule the world with a look."[2] This academic's posturing was not attractive. It made him look like a fool, but worse, it created an atmosphere shot through with ego, when the point of the proceedings was an exchange of ideas. What student would dare risk voicing an opinion in a context like this?

I think this brings us to another rule for the code, and this is that dignity matters, gravity counts. The people who are rewarded by the admiration economy must learn to behave themselves. They can't go around trying to "rule the world with a look." They must act with a certain dignity. They must display a certain self-possession. They must be circumspect. No showing off. No playing the fool. No entrancing entrances. No dramatic appearances. Oh, and Charlie, keep your pants on.

If you, Mr. Big Shot, make a show of your standing in the community, we know what will happen. People will withdraw their admiration. And then you will stop being useful. And then a man in Hill Top Homes will have to move back down into a rooming house and the company of predators. So cut us some slack and keep your ego in check.

Am I being cynical? Of course I am. I believe you have met human beings. I believe there's a very good chance you are a human being yourself. Which is to say you have ample evidence that we are monsters of vanity waiting to happen. Let's tap this for our social purposes. And let's endure the outcome. There is an eighty-year-old on a hilltop who doesn't care that we are uncomfortable. His discomfort is much worse.

Okay, how do we do this? How do we mobilize people who think it's enough to be law-abiding, self-supporting, and taxpaying? People who will not come to the aid of an eighty-year-old unless we can incent them with something more than the satisfaction of "giving back"? In Rowayton, Connecticut, with a population of 3,500 adults, we probably have five Bobs. What if we could do better than that? What if we could mobilize 1 percent of the town? What if we could recruit thirty-five Bobs? We would improve our "honor economy"—and our community—dramatically.

There might be a third cultural rule that gets in the way. Generally speaking, Americans are intensely egalitarian and we withhold our generosity from those we presume to be our "social betters." But Bob is not making a status claim of any kind. In fact, there is no status seeking about Bob. I'm sure he did handsomely in his professional life as an accountant. But you wouldn't know it from his lifestyle. He drives a Jeep. He dresses in Lands' End. His house is expensive because all the houses in this part of Connecticut are expensive. But nothing about his house invites the adjective *grand*. Some people in this part of the state cultivate a *haut bourgeois* style. (No Jeeps for them. They prefer Range Rovers that cost $100K.)

———

I found myself giving Bob spontaneous praise on one of our walks. The experiment had begun! (Or perhaps it's my "late-onset hyperbole" acting up again.) As my knowledge of his accomplishments began to accumulate, I remember suddenly looking at him and saying, "Geez, you're our Frank Capra." And it didn't cost me anything. And that's not because I have so much status that I can afford to give it away or because I am quick to engage in self-abasement. (I'm actually as self-important as the next guy. Probably worse.) Praising Bob felt like an easy thing to do. So why isn't it widespread?

To reward Bob, and incent more Bobs, we need to make his accomplishments public. Right now this knowledge travels, when it travels, by word of mouth. We can do better. When I thought about this problem, I recalled a feature of a beach club in town. They post the results of swimming races. On a board. Gold paint on lacquered wood. Little Bobby Liberman won the freestyle race in 1952! It's all there immortalized on wood.

Naturally, our option will be digital, not painted. We can show standings on our electronic bulletin board. (Our town has one on the Nextdoor platform called "Nextdoor Rowayton.") This will probably require a community curator, someone who monitors social streams, local chatter, and the community newsletter (*Rowayton Currents*). It will take a little effort to identify all the dimensions of accomplishment and to decide their relative weight. For the time being, we can do this "by hand." There will be many judgment calls. Eventually an algorithm will be called for, and that would help protect our curator from accusations of favoritism.

We could also use a kind of "prediction market" (aka "information market" or "decision market"). In this case, we give everyone a pretend hundred dollars and ask them to distribute these dollars across the candidates. We are now crowdsourcing the decision-making.

Okay, so we have identified Bobs. And we have publicized them. And we have generated a ranking. We have minted honor and distributed it. We may want to do more than merely show the outcome of our evaluation. Some ceremony may be called for. Perhaps a boozy dinner and a medal. But please, not an eight-year-old's soccer trophy. Let's make an effort.

Will this get a reaction? Will people compete for honor? That's exactly what we're hoping for. Will such competition be undignified? Who cares? In a perfect world, people would make generous gifts of time and effort to the community on their own. Inducements induce. Incentives incent. Before you know it, honor flows.

And what about a negative reaction to our honor economy? If the social scientific literature is correct, we should expect the formation of cliques and the emergence of curmudgeons. The latter are people who do nothing for the community. But they love to offer a noisy chorus of criticism. Until now, they have been largely unnoticed. But now that there is an honor culture in place, perhaps they will be a little more conspicuous.

Typically, curmudgeons protect themselves from judgment by denigrating the values that make them look bad. Their position is

"No, I don't help out in my community because a) it's all bullshit, b) this is the state's job, c) this is for busybodies, d) this is for grandstand- ers." Thus do they seek to absolve themselves from effort and from criticism. This is fine. Honor spreads out in the community. It ac- cumulates in some places and vanishes in others. This makes honor a light. Eventually, we will see the curmudgeons for who and what they are. Honor will find them out.

## Internal Honor

Okay, what about internal honor?

This is a very different creature. Where external honor is self- dramatizing, vain, and self-centered, internal honor is bookish and un- assuming. It is diffident, introverted, and usually indifferent to whether notice or recognition is forthcoming. But of course if the world insists on a Nobel Prize, it won't say no. (Unless it's Bob Dylan at his crank- iest). But otherwise, this honor is the perfect opposite of external honor. It does not wish to accrue value in an admiration economy. It just wants to be left alone.

Jim, the state trooper, used internal honor to create himself. In the process, he gave himself immunity against what other people think. An entire community or profession can doubt him or praise him, and that's okay. People can importune him. He does not flinch. Honor is its own arbiter. Honor is his armor.

This honor takes its strength from the fact that it is indifferent to public opinion and approval. It can choose its own goals. And it can keep at it even when the world disapproves. This is a fine quality to cultivate, because the world is good at disapproving.

On March 10, 2003, Natalie Maines of the Chicks, from a concert stage in London, said, "We're ashamed that the president of the United States is from Texas." Punishment was swift and unforgiving. Their number-one hit dropped from the charts. Radio stations refused to play their music. The Chicks had obscurity forced upon them. They refused to recant or apologize.

Alan Dershowitz was, until his recent retirement, a professor at Harvard Law. Late in his career, he took up unpopular positions in support of Israel, the Constitution, and President Donald Trump. The effect was striking.

> Now my family doesn't talk to me. People on the Vineyard don't talk to me. My wife was mad at me. . . . You know, one of the chapters in my new book is "The Cost of Trying to Live a Principled Life." And it's very, very hard to do. . . .[3]

I have a small experience of this. I decided early in my career to give up tenure and become a self-funding freelance anthropologist. I would no longer be answerable to academic committees or other anthropologists. Almost immediately, I began to drift out of anthropology's orthodoxy. My colleagues were furious. I was ridiculed. I was scorned. I was shunned. They didn't like where my ideas were going.

(God knows what they are going to think about this little exercise in applied anthropology! How dare I suggest our corrupt and corrupting culture can repair itself!) They insisted I was doing it for the money, that I had "sold out." They mounted an attack on my honor. For a touchy guy like me, this was not a pleasant experience. I don't like having my honor questioned, especially by a full professor who was making more money than me. (I have always spent my consulting riches on research.)

So what was I going to do? Change? Cave? Internal honor prevented me. It secured me. I thought, *The research data is clear. Anthropologists have been mostly wrong when it comes to the study of their own culture. Their elitism and their ideologies prevent them from seeing it clearly.* Revealing this truth seemed to me more important than the esteem of my peers. I persevered. Naturally, honor was my armor.

Internal honor says, "Read your own compass, make your own way, do not hew to the party line." It is often wrong, and it is always redundant.

By the look of things, the Chicks and Alan Dershowitz took criticism bravely. They were unwavering. I took it less well, and several times a failure of confidence brought me low. And this is what impressed me about Jim the state trooper. His self-possession was formidable. You talked to him for even a brief while and you thought, *This guy is indestructible. Nobody can touch this guy.*

I never did discover where Jim's honor came from. There's no evidence that he read Epictetus or the Stoics. He was not obviously the beneficiary of a modern self-help philosophy. Jim's moral compass was forged in part by his training in that stronghold of honor, the military. As for the rest, it's not clear. As near as I can tell, Jim created it for himself. This was do-it-yourself honor.

There is a problem, too. A person who is driven by internal honor can actually fall so far out of the orbit of popular opinion that she ceases to be useful and becomes perhaps even dangerous. It's good to be self-motivating, but much less good to be a kook. And these days, especially in a culture that has lost many of its mainstays, it is really very easy to begin inventing your own reality. You begin to march to your own drummer, and before you know it, you are building a cabin in Montana and writing manifestos. So the person driven by internal honor has to know what other people think, even as she presses on with her own vision of things.

Everyone will have their own internal honor, even as we all subscribe to the same external honor economy. This means we must each examine our soul and figure out what we really stand for, as qualified by what we are really good at, as qualified by where the need is greatest. If and when this puts us up against conventional thinking and received wisdom, we are going to have to decide whether we can take the criticism and the discouragement and even the infamy that come our way. Are we prepared to pay the price for an unpopular position? Can we survive the scorn? Can we take it? The answer in a Hollywood film is always—cue rising orchestral music—"Yes, yes, and yes." But in real life, we all have different tolerances. And some internal honor may prove too pricey, too punishing for our particular constitutions. Choose wisely. Bite off only slightly more than you can chew. And then—cue music—rise to the occasion that internal honor supplies.

## Roles and Rules

We can imagine a Charlie Rose, staring at an attractive reporter across the desk and entertaining lunatic propositions on the order of "Maybe she likes me," "Maybe she likes older men," or "You know, I am pretty damn attractive." Poor Charlie. A Victorian morality was clear on this point. It said, "The rules are specified by your roles. You are a producer. She is a reporter. Do your job as the rulebook defines it." It would be good to return to that clarity, wouldn't it?

Unless compromised by privation or injustice, a Victorian could count on clarity. Roles were clear. As a male, you were defined as a father, son, citizen, subject, employer, employee, soldier, devotee, believer, belonger, adherent. Each of these roles had rules, and the rules regarding each were clear (and surprisingly redundant).

What Victorians hoped for was a "sincere" performance of these social roles and rules. This meant believing in—and committing to—the social identities assigned to them. The aggregate effect was magical. Social life was organized as if by a magnetic field. Yes, of course there was failure and bad behavior. (Consult Charles Dickens for the details.) But, generally speaking, there was clarity. People knew who they were, how to act, what they owed and to whom. They did not need to be clergymen or moral philosophers. What they needed to know was already etched into their view of the world. It was etched into their sense of self.

Gradually, Lionel Trilling tells us, roles and rules were challenged by a new cultural objective.[4] What mattered more than the sincerity of our social performance was authenticity of the self. Socially assigned identities were now seen to be problematic. They were no longer regarded as potent distillations of moral knowledge. Now they were falsehoods imposed from on high. Americans had a new charge: discover the essential self . . . and if that meant forsaking roles and rules, well, so be it.

Trilling argued that American culture was now host to an "adversary impulse." A range of social critics was newly influential. In chapter 4, we glimpsed some of them. The Parisian bohemians, American novelists, Beat poets, hippies, punks, and a perennial avant-garde all heaped scorn on roles and rules and the "prison" of bourgeois conformity.[5]

This shift in the polarity of American culture made for many differences. And it certainly changed the moral compass. Scorn for roles meant scorn for rules. The magnetic field began to break up. Jailbreak followed. Americans were unbound, now all free to discover the Charlie Rose within.

American selfhood was taking on new properties, new dynamics. Where once it sought roles and rules, now it looked for the truth in experience and self-discovery. This changed the way we thought about emotion. For Elizabethan humanists, emotions were a source of irrationality. For the new culture, they were messages from our hidden selves. The first approach said, "Suppress them." The new one said, "Own them," "Act on them," even when it meant engaging in dubious behavior. Daring became less daring. Now it was obligatory. You had to be pathbreaking all the time.

The new selfhood had 4WD, so to speak. It had off-road capability. The idea was to get away from the conventional definitions of self and life, leave the beaten track, and open new paths of self-discovery. Drugs, therapy, meditation—all of these were opportunities for enlightenment. All of them lead away from roles and rules.

Is the new self the fundamental cause of our instability? I don't think so. The last thing I mean to suggest is that honor requires us to roll back the individualism of the twentieth century. (People do try this, and I sympathize with the impulse. But let's be clear, it always fails because it is fundamentally at odds with what and where our culture is.) The "adversary" regime did blur some of the old clarities, but on balance it improved us.

But we now really have a problem. All that experimenting left us with a muddy moral universe. Wrong behavior is less clearly defined, and therefore less obviously wrong. So we need new clarity. One way to create an honorable workplace is to insist that roles have rules.

This would have made Charlie Rose's world much clearer. Charlie would have felt tempted by a young intern, paused, and then consulted the role-rule book. He would have found a passage that said something like, "Bosses in the world of work are supposed to instruct, support, and encourage their subordinates." And acted accordingly. A clear-cut rule such as this would have spared his interns the sense that they were living in an honorless world. It would have spared them the ugliness of a world in which "people said what they wanted to you, people did what they wanted to you."[6]

Some human resources departments have made this rule explicit by asserting that when colleagues are working in the same building for the same company, there really shouldn't be any extra-professional contact at all. Maybe a celebratory drink after work once a year. But that's all.

But more often there's no explicit rendering of role-rules. But this is easily fixed. With a little encouragement, we could ask people to consult their sense of "decency." "Oh," I can hear someone protest, "you are now smuggling in the very thing you claim we do not have." And that someone has a point. I am smuggling in the very thing I claim has disappeared. If our moral compass is broken, the really bad actors have no decency within to summon.

So how to do this? Let's resort to one of our most ancient moral staples: the Golden Rule. This has a beautiful simplicity to it. It says, "Do unto others as you want them to do unto you." This does not require a moral stipulation. It merely says, "Ask yourself if you would want to be treated the way you now contemplate treating an intern." In Charlie Rose's case this leaves us with a very clear injunction. "Charlie," it says, "would you wish to be groped in the hallway? Well? Or would you want to find yourself in a room with a boss wearing a bath towel?" The Golden Rule comes with its own inescapably obvious instructional manual. No moral calculations are actually required.

## Shame and Lance Armstrong

Americans are a forgiving bunch. With enough contrition and penance on the part of people who behave badly, we say, "Oh, that's okay. Welcome back." We are especially forgiving of politicians. In the well-chosen words of journalist Jack Shafer, "Washington routinely forgives its philanderers, drug addicts and alcoholics, embezzlers, perjurers, bribers and bribees, liars, burglars and tax evaders, granting them the redemption of another term in office or a job in a lobbying shop or think tank after their scandal passes."[7]

Perhaps we need to change this. Perhaps it's time to resurrect shame. It won't be easy. In a therapeutic culture, shame is a shameful thing. It is seen to inflict a terrible injury on selfhood—so terrible that we feel, generally speaking, that it shouldn't be used as a means of punishment. It's just wrong.

Shame has fallen out of fashion. We're now a little embarrassed that we ever cared so much about it. We're ashamed of shame. Guilt, now that's something we are more comfortable with. It's less extravagant, less punishing, less theatrical. Best of all, it's more private. Guilt is inward-facing. Shame shouts out.

This is why shame belongs to an honor culture. Honor gives us a social reputation. Shame takes it away. Summarily. Without a hearing. All of a sudden. With prejudice.

Did the Jeffrey Epsteins, Charlie Roses, and Harvey Weinsteins of the world feel guilt? Maybe, maybe not. But in their better moments, they must certainly have felt shame. Whether they like it or not, we cover them in shame.

The therapeutic community disapproves of this. It says shame is a tragic condition, that it is an attack on self-esteem. It feeds our addictions. It inflicts a debilitating wound. People can recover from guilt, the argument goes, but they may never get over shame. Or, in the words of clinical specialist Megan Bronson, "Guilt says a behavior is not okay while shame says that we innately are not okay."[8]

So shame has been shuffled off the public stage. Sure, we call people "shameless." We say people should be "ashamed" of themselves. But shame as an instrument of outrage? We hardly use it at all.

We could shame drug dealers. But we don't. We could shame corrupt civic employees, but we don't do that, either. We should really shame telemarketers. (In my opinion, Guantánamo is too good for telemarketers.) It's as if shame is too obvious, too biblical, too much like Shakespeare as they played it in the nineteenth century, all blood and thunder. We like to think we are subtler, more forgiving now. Shame is a public hanging in a time when we prefer a stinging dose of reproach.

But what if shame is actually a good thing? What if shame deserves a comeback? Yes, it's crude. But so is honor. It's not about understanding your essential goodness or feeling your pain. It's not about giving you the benefit of the doubt. Honor is dangerous. Shame is your punishment.

It might even be useful if shame were like pain. Pain is a mechanical signal. It says, "Stop doing what you are doing." No thoughtful self-scrutiny is called for. Something just hurts. "Oh," we say, "I should probably stop that. And get medical attention."

What if shame sent a signal of its own? It stabs our moral sense to let us know that something has happened and we should stop. And seek philosophical attention.

It's not clear that Charlie Rose had a shame reflex. Millions of employers and employees apparently cannot see what they should not do. No reflex interrupts their behavior. Nothing stabs at their better sense.

## Did Shame Kill Crack?

There is one stunning precedent. Some decades ago, shame came to our rescue. It intervened and changed behavior. It came to the aid of the American city, and the millions of people living there.

Crack was an innovation created to solve an oversupply problem. There was too much cocaine in American cities. So someone figured out that if you removed the hydrochloride from cocaine and heated it to the melting point, the result could be smoked. This made it safer to manufacture than freebase cocaine and faster-working than ordinary cocaine. Plus, and most strikingly, crack was so powerful it made cocaine feel like a mint julep at a garden party.

By 1990, crack was well established, and people were properly terrified. Certain parts of New York were uninhabitable, gang wars broke out, bullets flew, noncombatants were constantly in harm's way, and drug lords actually threatened to assume control of neighborhoods in

Harlem, Washington Heights, and Brooklyn. The city was now threatened by an overwhelming "drug tide."[9]

New York fought back with more convictions and longer sentences. The city's police made some three hundred thousand crack-related arrests over ten years.

But not everyone thinks that it was police work that made the difference. Indeed, some people think that crack was waning even before these tougher measures kicked in.

Dr. Ric Curtis is a cultural anthropologist at John Jay College of Criminal Justice in Manhattan. In the course of his research, he has talked to more than a thousand crack users and dealers. His conclusion: "Drug markets were in contraction well before the stepped-up police action."[10]

So what happened? What shifted crack? This is a drug so powerful it appears to be for some people instantly addicting and so powerful that rehabilitation is near impossible.[11]

Shame. It might have been shame.

It turns out that addicts hated being addicts. Crack was a humiliating thing. Journalist Timothy Egan talked to Selena Jones, a Harlem resident whose mother was a chronic crack user. Ms. Jones said,

If you were raised in a house where somebody was a crack addict, you wanted to get as far away from that drug as you could. People look down on them so much that even crack-heads don't want to be crackheads anymore.[12]

The drug dealers scorned their clients. Egan talked to an addict named Thomas Covington who had noticed what Ms. Jones had noticed. Addicts were ashamed of themselves in a way heroin and cocaine addicts were not.

> [S]tarting in the early 90's, Mr. Covington said, he noticed a shift in the attitudes of young drug dealers. "They didn't use crack," he said. "And they didn't respect people who did. To me, being a 34 or 35-year-old guy, standing on line and handing my money to a 15-year-old, that was humiliating."

Crack was disfiguring. Addicts didn't care what they looked like or smelled like. People lost their families. At the height of crack's popularity, at least ten thousand children were taken from addicted parents and put in the foster care system.[13]

But the most vicious punishment was shame. And shame was so intense it actually was enough to liberate people from crack's ferocious grip.

Shame intervened in the lives of people who were otherwise an absolute misery to themselves, their families, and their communities. It helped eliminate a culture of crime and criminality. Most poignantly, shame came to the aid of children taken from their families. Shame was actually more powerful than crack. And that's saying something.

We punish celebrities with a tepid shame. And this means giving them *looks*. Sneering looks. Scornful looks. The celeb was once greeted with "OMG Charlie Rose!" Now the greeting is often "Ewwww, I think that's Charlie Rose. Can we get another table, please?" This is merely shame lite.

Celebrities can always find an outer ring of supporters who are so desperate to be in the company of someone famous they will seek even corrupt celebrity. And they will come to the celeb's emotional aid, scorning the scorners as hopeless, small-minded losers. "Who cares what they think. I mean, you don't, right, Charlie? I mean, tell me you don't care what those losers think." But of course, Charlie *does* care. He is embarrassed by the people who will keep him company. He's ashamed of *them*.

This is good for starters, but what we need is a heavyweight, machine-grade, industrial-strength shame that so punishes the guilty that they will think twice before giving it an opportunity to enter their lives and ruin their social reputation. We need something that stalks the guilty party, that diminishes him, that make him ridiculous in the eyes of his peers and the public.

American culture in the nineteenth century experienced shame in this way. And then things changed. Somehow, we decided that a person could do quite terrible things and eventually, after an apology tour or two, all would be forgiven. Your rehabilitation would be granted. Your celebrity would be renewed.

The reason the therapeutic community dislikes shame is precisely that it *is* so punishing. To quote Bronson again, "Guilt says a behavior is not okay while shame says that we innately are not okay."

I'm okay with this. When Charlie Rose grabs an intern, it is *more* than the behavior that's not okay. It's Charlie Rose. Something is wrong with Charlie Rose. Innately. So let's let shame send a signal. Charlie, if you do this, you are innately not okay.

I am sure some shame, maybe half of all shame, *is* debilitating. Honestly, I don't care. If this gives us shame that's powerfully corrective, I say that's an acceptable trade-off. Does that seem a little brutal? Does that seem a little primitive, retrograde, backward sliding in the therapeutic scheme of things? Let's ask the women preyed upon by Harvey Weinstein. I'm betting they would accept the trade-off, too.

Guilt is not enough. It's merely cocaine. We need something stronger. We need something as powerful as crack. Shame is a useful social emotion because it threatens the removal of standing. And this says to Harvey Weinstein, "Behave like this and you put your standing, authority, and wealth at risk. Act like this, and you are out." Actually, this is what happened to Weinstein, but it took a court of law to accomplish this. Without successful prosecution, Weinstein would still be pleading for understanding.

Shame works even on those who are not famous. It threatens everyone's social standing. After all, we all get some honor as table stakes. We are all spotted some small amount of honor, so we have something to lose and something to augment. It may not be much, but it's enough to make us think twice. Perhaps shame deserves to be restored to the world. It's a very effective way to correct the behavior of men like Weinstein and protect women like his victims.

Sometimes we want judgment. Something almost biblical.

## The Rip Van Winkle Scenario

Falling into a deep slumber in the sixteenth century, summoned only for episodic and cameo appearances since, honor comes fully awake in the present day and regards America in the opening moments of the twenty-first century. It appears before us in the form of Sir Thomas Elyot.[14] Think of him as honor incarnate.

At first, everything's a blur. In fact, Sir Thomas does not recognize much of our world. It's all so fast-moving and frenetic.

Sir Thomas's portal proves to be the East Village of Manhattan. On Second Avenue, to be specific, not far from McSorley's Old Ale House. Sir Thomas wanders for a while and eventually finds himself on the steps of something he recognizes. Yes, this is a church, he's sure of it. It says "Middle Collegiate Church" right on it. Sir Thomas steps tentatively in. It's early on a Wednesday morning, so things are quiet. He picks up a brochure.

> Middle Church is where therapy meets Broadway; where art
> and dance meet a gospel revival; where old time religion gets
> a new twist. We are Bach, Beatles, and Beethoven; we are jazz,

hip-hop, and spirituals. We are inspired by Howard Thurman, Ruby Sales, Fannie Lou Hamer, and Martin Luther King. We are on-your-feet worship and take-it-to-the-streets activism. We feed the hungry and work for a living wage; we fight for LGBTQ equality and march for racial/ethnic justice. We stand up for the stranger and the immigrant; we care for women's lives and Mother Earth.[15]

Sir Thomas blinks. He tucks the pamphlet into his gown. He will look at this later.

People begin to filter in. There must be a noon service. Sir Thomas doesn't feel conspicuous, despite the fact he is wearing the Tudor flat cap that is roughly five hundred years out of fashion. In fact, no one is paying him the least bit of attention. No one is tipping their hat. No one is nodding in acknowledgment, let alone wonder, let alone awe. (I mean, really.)

What's odder still is that these frenetic Americans do not even defer to one another. It's everyone for him- and herself. Sir Thomas can't find any sign of the hierarchy that keeps things tidy. An idea begins to dawn. "Oh, you Americans got rid of hierarchy." There is a tone of astonishment, as if to say, "How in God's name did you pull that off?" In Sir Thomas's world, there is no order that is not hierar-chical.[16]

Americans are egalitarian, in theory, at least. Differences flourish. People do not sit high and low in the larger scheme of things, not consistently, not essentially, not for long. Sir Thomas shakes his head.

To create a social world without hierarchy? That's a magician's trick. That's sorcerer's work.

For the old honor system, hierarchy provided beautifully articulated chains of leadership and obedience. Those who ranked high presumed to advise those who ranked low, and those who ranked low accepted obedience as their duty. Sir Thomas looks at us and smiles. Apparently, we let every individual chart their own course, free of superordinates' advice. *Good luck with that*, he thinks.

Sir Thomas begins to see our ambitions go further still. Not only do we not assign rank, but we long ago dispensed with a single set of categories with which to keep things tidy. We are unashamedly heterogeneous. We have a bewildering variety of religious and moral beliefs. We have a plenitude of ways of being. We have multiplied even our definitions of gender and age and lifestyle. Before you know it, you are all "Broadway meets therapy" and the Middle Collegiate Church. Sir Thomas is still standing there, staring up at the stained glass he recognizes and the congregation he does not. It's all so very un-sixteenth-century!

Sir Thomas is getting it now. Americans are so very various there *can't* be a single moral agenda. There can't be a "one size" that fits all. Everyone is *obliged* to make their own way.

Sir Thomas shakes his head, as if to say, "Wow, anything you can do to make things harder, that's precisely what you do, isn't it?"

And then he sets to work looking for the bigger picture. (As a time traveler, he has exceptional powers of pattern detection.) He notices that we have demoted some of our moral leaders and social experts.

Even those who continue to have influence don't have anything like authority. In an intensely individualistic world, their advice is optional. Honor sees that we no longer attend our churches and synagogues as often as we once did. The university world is well stocked with experts, but their moral authority is limited. (Just as well.)

Sir Thomas can see the moral compass spinning wildly. And, frankly, he can't believe we let it get this bad. That we actually managed to let common sense and common decency run down. Apparently, we assumed they were endowments that would always be there, that they were resources people could draw upon even in the absence of moral leadership. But eventually even these began to falter. And here's the astonishing part: we still did nothing.

And then comes the really astounding revelation. Thomas shakes his head as if to say, "Wow, you people." The big revelation is that we let monsters roam. Honor has read *Beowulf*. (He borrowed a copy from Lawrence Nowell, the Dean of Lichfield.) And he can't help feeling that what he's looking at here is chaos. Larry Nassar. Jerry Sandusky. Harvey Weinstein. Honor is horrified. "You gave them power. And you let them prey upon your athletes, your children, and your actors. For years! *Years!* If you are looking for an indictment of American culture, this is it. You let monsters loose and let them roam."

Sir Thomas believes the latitude these monsters were granted, in turn, encouraged smaller monsters. The bandits and the scoundrels, the ones who thought, *Hey, you know, maybe I could get away with this after all. Why not try? Let's just see.* And before you know it, you have people installing locks on the office door. Honor is impressed with the sheer scale of our stupidity. "Now you were in the clutches of a circular causality that eventually became a downward spiral! Bad behavior set low standards, which produced still worse behavior, which unleashed big monsters, which unleashed small ones, until American culture was a deeply dangerous place. Good going."

Sir Thomas is right. We stood by and watched things come undone. Moral schemes that took thousands of years to create lost their hold on us. We drifted into uncharted waters. There were some appeals for a return to religion, to morality, to goodness.[17] But mostly we just stood there.

Sir Thomas looks at us. He says, "And by the end of the twentieth century, you were lost. With a few honorable exceptions, no one seemed prepared to sound the alarm. You were looking at a steady state of dissolution. And you did nothing."

We hem and we haw. We were busy, okay? Finally we resort to that gifted rhetorical tactician, Jeff Lebowski (aka the Dude in *The Big Lebowski*), who might have said, "It was complicated, man. We had a lot going on." And it all happened so gradually, with a couple of very steep downturns, like the '70s and early '80s. Then things seemed to get better. We thought, *Figure out broken windows and graffiti, and the rest will take care of itself.* We were wrong.

Sir Thomas is a fair man. He notes our accomplishments. We began the hard work of tearing down some of our most noxious institutions: racism, sexism, ageism, ableism, and xenophobia. We helped some individuals get out from under social conventions that denied them a place in the creative sun, that withered them with skepticism, that filled them with anxiety, that denied them confidence and opportunity. "That was good," Sir Thomas says. "You did well there."

And in some ways, Sir Thomas actually likes what we have done for honor. No one gets honor as a gift of birth or social standing. That always struck him as too easy. And a little insulting. Like honor was a party favor, to be handed out to some and arbitrarily withheld from others.

"So how do you get honor?" Sir Thomas asks. "You have to earn it, I guess."

This is really awkward.

"No," we say. "You don't have to earn it. We don't actually think you need to have it at all."

There is a long pause.

Sir Thomas looks at us carefully. This could be a prank. Elizabethans liked a good "jape."

"You what?"

"We don't feel people need honor, really. It's just . . . It's complicated, okay? We have a lot going on."

When you resort to the Dude defense, your argument is . . . well, you don't really have an argument. At that point, you're just making stuff up.

Honor can see this.

"Listen, tell me that you made an assessment. Surely you could see you were creating more bad than good. Right? That bad was winning and must eventually triumph. You turned your world upside down, and forgot about me."

There's a long silence.

Sir Thomas speaks again.

"You broke down all the things that were wrong with my world, the cruelties of class and status, the suppression of talent; you stripped away false gods and corrupt morality; you made the self multiple and fluid. And you thought order would take care of itself? You forgot about honor."

So let's go to the code.

# CHAPTER 7

## The New Honor Code

1. **Honor honor.**

   Start by taking honor seriously. Treat it as something real and tangible. Think of it like money—something that can be gained and lost, saved and invested, managed and leveraged. Honor is a currency. Treat it as carefully as you would any store of value. In those endless ads on TV, we are encouraged to think about our credit score. Think about your honor score.

2. **Treasure the honor you have.**

   You get some honor just for showing up. Everyone does. What now? Some people squander this honor straightaway. They act selfishly. They diminish others. They damage the common good. Others cultivate and augment their honor. Keep what you have. Keep your "starter honor." Build from there.

   If, by the time you are fifteen, you still have only your starter honor, well, that's bad. If, by the time you are, say, eighteen, you don't even have your starter honor, that's when a capital *L* begins to take shape on your forehead and you can forget going to the college of your choice. (Colleges have a variety of ways of assessing admission candidates. It's time for them to measure honor, too.)

**3. Find your roles, find your rules.**

Some honor comes from being true to the roles we assume in life. We are someone's parent, husband/wife, boss, colleague, employee, coach, neighbor. Each of our roles comes with a set of rules.

Specifying roles is relatively easy. Who are the people in our domestic, neighborhood, professional worlds? What part do we play relative to each of them? Identify the people you know, and finish the sentence "I am his or her *x*." Easy.

Now comes the hard part. We need to specify the rules for each role. Some of these are vague. That's your new job. Make them crisp.

Some of this is pretty obvious. Married partners owe one another mutual aid and respect. Teachers and students, employees and employers, consultants and clients. All of these have a handbook written by HR. Perhaps not quite a brilliant guide. But surely good enough for the likes of some of our worst monsters.

Some things are less clear. What about honesty in a

relationship? Do we owe honesty? How much honesty do we owe? I am laissez-faire when it comes to honesty. I think white lies are okay. Indeed, I believe that the only way we survive certain moments in a relationship (and many of the moments in the COVID-19 era) is by holding our tongue. Only the diplomatic can hope to stay married. So white lies are tolerable. Each relationship will establish its own expectations and tolerances.

What about fidelity? Every marriage ceremony demands this of us. It's there in the contract. But the threat of *infidelity* is always with us, and for some people lines blur. And they can't. Fidelity is not renegotiable, except by explicit and mutual agreement. Otherwise, we have to be scrupulous. We have to be honorable.

One way to specify rules is to talk about them with other people who hold the same role. I think women are practiced and skillful at this—men much less so. That diminishes clarity. Some men have never talked to other men about roles—not their fathers, not their friends. And a lot of men will insist on, let's call it, "sly dog" chatter when it comes to something like infidelity. But unless they are scoundrels, eventually they will sober up and take on the task at hand. We owe our spouses fidelity. Sometimes it helps to say this out loud.

When things are really vague, there is a backup plan. Use the Golden Rule. When Harvey Weinstein abused an actress, he may have defended himself with the insane idea that he was merely playing "the Hollywood game." But the Golden Rule says, "Harvey, before you remove your pants in the presence of an actress and demand sexual services you must answer this question: What would you think if you were so treated? If there is any sign of asymmetry, then calling it 'the Hollywood game' is a dodge. It's not a game. It's not an agreement. It's not an arrangement. It's predation."

Anytime we find ourselves working on a rationale that absolves us from following the rules, that's when we are obliged to say, "Wait a second, is anyone else rewriting the rules of this role? And in what spirit do I seek to rewrite the rules of this role?" And if there is any evidence that you are looking for a way out of the rule, there is a simple expedient, a useful phrase. Repeat after me: "Snap out of it." There is no sneaking out of honor. If you wish to rewrite the rules that bind you, you must do so explicitly, and with the full knowledge of the person to whom you are bound by role. In Weinstein's case, this might have meant a hand-printed sign on his door at Miramax, "Anyone entering this office to seek advice or assistance from Mr. Harvey Weinstein must understand that Mr. Weinstein will treat your presence as an implicit signal that you are prepared to provide sexual services as part of the deal. Have a nice day."

4. **Cultivate your external honor.**

Our external honor is the reputation that precedes us. It comes to us thanks to our good behavior. There is a simple test of our external honor: what happens when our name comes up in a conversation? If in every possible conversation everyone draws a blank, we have no honor.

We create this honor by creating some good for some people in some community. This doesn't mean that we have to do Meals on Wheels—though it wouldn't hurt. We can be a pillar of our book club, the person who convenes, reminds, schedules, keeps track. Do something useful. Do it well. Do it reliably. Do it for the right reasons. We approach honor on baby steps. It doesn't take a lot to get started.

Earning honor doesn't have to be selfless. It's enough to be a good and honest carpenter, investment counselor, librarian. But great honor is usually selfless. We have done all the things required of lower-order honor. We showed up. We satisfied everything expected of us according to our roles and occupations. And then some of us went one big step further. We created some extraordinary good. But notice, if we do great things to win honor, it must still be thrust upon us. Honor isn't something we take. It's something we are given by others.

Notice that external honor has nothing to do with wealth, status, or power. (These are measures of something, but not of honor.) In fact, sometimes the pursuit of wealth, status, and power *costs us* honor. It prompts us to do things that are dishonorable. Sometimes we have to choose.

We are now publicly traded. We have entered the honor economy. How much honor accrues to us will depend on our efforts and the value of these efforts as "traded" on a public exchange. This means that if everyone in my little town in Connecticut is acting like Bob, it is going to take extra effort to achieve Bob status. Economies are beautifully responsive systems for discovering and distributing value. They will discover and distribute honor, too.

5. **Cultivate your internal honor.**
We also create honor by creating some good for some people in some community. But in this case, we take our bearings not from a collective determination of what matters but our own, sometimes deeply private, sense of what counts. This is where we stop caring about what our neighbors think. This is where we consult our souls.

The goal of internal honor could be achieved with the help of our pastor or rabbi. Or we might find a guru of one kind or another who is prepared to shape our moral sense of things. But more often, it comes from deep within us. We know what matters. And we are prepared to pursue it, even if no one agrees with us.

No one is giving us credit. Indeed, the more our goal departs from the common view of things, the more dishonor is likely to accrue. This means internal honor is something we will have to confer upon ourselves. We can expect to work for free. No one is going to compensate us for work they don't see the point of. This might be the most honorable honor. Thankless honor might be the gold standard.

We are the arbiters of our own value. The community can turn against us, or someone can decide we are a bad person, but our internal honor protects us. The trick is to have a sober, contemplative, rigorous, unflinching discussion with ourselves. If we believe we did the right thing, we have honor. And it doesn't matter what others think. Honor is our armor.

This aspect of honor is important because it prevents us from chasing honor by doing the things others think are honorable. We do honorable things for their own sake, not because we will win praise, power, status, or money. We do good things because they are good.

Some time ago I interviewed a woman living on a farm in Iowa. She had crafted her own objectives in life. One of these was to befriend a young woman who was bereft of parents and a little lost. My Iowa respondent had experienced precisely this kind of childhood herself. So she knew what to do, and why it mattered. "Everyone needs someone who thinks they are wonderful. Just one," she told me. She did this without recognition.

6. **Augment the honor of others.**

We must praise others. And a lot of us are reluctant to do this for the "zero-sum" reasons discussed above. We believe that what we give to others, we take from ourselves. But honor economies are generative economies. The more there is, the more there is. And the more there is, the better.

The idea is to praise people. This is not about flattery. We are not trading compliments. We are not trying to make people feel good about themselves (or good about us). This is not about "liking" someone's tweet, post, or photo. This is not about celebrity. When it comes to honor, most celebrities have nothing to teach us.

And it may well be that our praise may turn some people into insufferable fools. Too bad. We will just have to suffer them. It's the price we pay.

7. **Do not diminish the honor of others.**

There is always a temptation to scorn, diminish, criticize, or belittle others. Humans do this for a variety of reasons. None of them is worthy.

When we diminish others, we starve our community of a precious thing, of the honor that moves people to do good.

When we gossip and indulge in rumor, we steal someone's dignity and we diminish their honor. Attacking someone's honor is a special class of crime. It attacks the very root of our community. When we diminish the honor of others, we threaten to extinguish our own.

This is bad news for some people in particular, for those who love being petty and trading in insults. And it's bad news for those who are now the illegitimate recipients of honor, the stuffed-shirt brigade. We should probably withhold honor from the timeservers, the people who work the system, the people who always take the safe option instead of the promising one. No one should win honors merely for having served their term. And we should be vigilant when the people getting the honors are the people who mint them.

Gossipers are the opposite of counterfeiters. Instead of putting false value into circulation, they are taking real value out. They are starving us of a precious resource.

8. **Your honor is not durable, but delicate. Once it's damaged, it's damaged. Once it's gone, it's gone.**

I think it's plausible to assume that Matt Lauer is plotting his return to air. Someone is going to have to tell him, "Matt! I have bad news. You, sir, are done." We have politicians who lied about serving in Vietnam, and they are still in office. We have journalists who lied about seeing action in the field, and they are back on the air. This sends a terrible message. It says there is no cost to disreputable behavior. But once we restore honor as a thing in the world, there is no point to plotting our return to the air. We are obliged to say, "Matt Lauer, you had honor. We trusted you. You destroyed your honor. Now we don't trust you. Go. Just go." Only thus does a Walter Cronkite get the honor he deserves. At the end of forty years of service, he was manifestly a figure who defined and advanced the field of journalism. Honor gets its due.

In the worst cases, if need be, we will have to resort to shame. The honor economy says there are no second chances. There are no apology tours. No "Please forgive me." No "You can't blame me. I'm the real victim here." Actually, we *can* blame you and we will. If you want to carry on as a celebrity, behave yourself.

9. **Be an honor architect.**

The honor economy needs a stock exchange. It needs people who are prepared to build the infrastructure through which honor flows, accumulating with some, fleeing from others. We need people to help build and monitor these exchanges.

We have seen several remarkable social networks established in the past twenty years. These have brought fame (and sometimes infamy) to figures like Mark Zuckerberg, Jack Dorsey, and Reid Hoffman. We need more pioneers like this, people who are prepared to build networks that make clear who has honor and who does not. Or perhaps we could simply build an overlay that adds an honor score to Facebook, Twitter, and LinkedIn. Honor needs a template.

And then there are those who are struggling to find and build their internal honor. These people must welcome advisors and counselors who can give advice. Most internal honor is pursued on a DIY basis. But I wish now, looking back, that I had asked someone to give me advice regarding my pursuit of internal honor when I was young. Why did I think I needed to make it such a lonely, desperate vigil? I didn't. DIY honor is good. DIYWALH honor (do it yourself with a little help) is even better.

10. **Rinse and repeat, as necessary.**
    Honor is a discipline. Honor is a practice. Honor gets better with experience. And our ways and means and goals should probably shift constantly. We will need to stop from time to time and take stock of our honor accomplishments. And recalibrate. And, when necessary, renovate with the tireless energy of a Bob Vila or the Property Brothers.

# ACKNOWLEDGMENTS

Many people have contributed to this book, by giving inspiration on the page or in conversation. No one listed here read the manuscript or in any way approved of it. All errors of fact and judgment belong to the author. The following people are blameless.

Devout thanks to: Michaels Adams, David Alworth, George Anastaplo, David Armour, Sylvia Augaitis, Thomas Ball, Sam Balsy, the Bergmans, Jennifer Bermingham, Bob Boland, Emily Carleton, Kevin Clark, Wendy Clark, Pip Coburn, Edward Cotton, Lindan Courtemanche, John Cruickshank, Noah Cruickshank, Christian Crumlish, Lauren Culbertson, Russell Davies, the DeCesares, Colin Drummond, Colette Dublois, Irina Alexandra Dumitrescu, Mark Earls, Bob Eydt, Tracy Fellows, Rob Fields, Melissa Fisher, Gerry Flahive, Sam Ford, the Goodmans, Pryce Greenow, Ric Grefe, Tom Guarriello, Robert Hall, Jeannette Hanna, Jodie Harris, Doug Hattaway, Barbara Holzapfel, Andrea Hunt, Alfred Ironside, Jan Kestle, Robert Kincaide, Justin Kirby, Leora Kornfeld, Joan Kron, Rabbi Irwin Kula, Richard Laermer, Jeanne Lam, Drew Lamm, Guy Lanou, Peter Lay-wine, Anne Lewison, Rick Liebling, Ed Liebow, Wendell and Tom Livingston, John Lowry, Heather MacLean, Diana Magana, Marilyn Maitland, Tyler Maitland, Timothy Malefyt, Brett Marchard, Michael Margolis, W. David Marx, Kevin McCuistion, Daryl McCullough, Emmet McCusker, Joe and Christine Melchione, David and Betsy Mettler, Alan Middleton, Robert Morais, Eric Nehrlich, Jerry Nevins, Bill O'Connor, Bree Omule, Bill O'Neil, Harriet O'Neil, Chris Perry, Joan Peterdi, Molly Pigeon, Thomas Pigeon, Fred Popp, Virginia Postrel, Leo Rayman, Monica Ruffo, Richard Sheer, Lenore Skenazy, Catherine Smith, Jonathan Smith, Stephanie Smith, Sharlene Sones, Ruth Sonius, Tim Sullivan, Patti Sunderland, Anne Sutherland, Cheryl Swanson, Wodek Szemberg, Marta Tellado, Gillian Tett, Sophie Wade, Polly Watson, V. Werenko Keller, Marilyn Wiles-Kettenmann, Sara Winge, and Wendy Yaross.

# NOTES

## INTRODUCTION

1. Lenore Skenazy, *Free-Range Kids: Giving Our Children the Freedom We Had Without Going Nuts with Worry* (San Francisco: Jossey-Bass, 2009).

2. "Jennie's Family History," TV commercial, Ancestry.com, 2019, 30 sec.

## CHAPTER 1: SYMPTOMS OF AN HONOR SHORTAGE

1. C. Ramsey Fahs, "2012 Harvard Men's Soccer Team Produced Sexually Explicit 'Scouting Report' on Female Recruits," *Harvard Crimson*, October 25, 2016, http://www.thecrimson.com/article/2016/10/25/harvard-mens-soccer-2012-report/.

2. Andrew M. Duehren, C. Ramsey Fahs, and Daphne C. Thompson, "Harvard Cancels Men's Soccer Season After Finding Sexually Explicit 'Reports' Continued Through 2016," *Harvard Crimson*, November 4, 2016, http://www.thecrimson.com/article/2016/11/4/soccer-suspended-scouting-report-harvard/.

3. Fahs, "Harvard Men's Soccer Team Produced Sexually Explicit 'Scouting Report.'"

4. The Members of the 2016 Harvard Men's Soccer Team, "An Apology from Harvard Men's Soccer," *Harvard Crimson*, November 4, 2016, https://www.thecrimson.com/article/2016/11/4/mens-soccer-apology.

5. Hannah Natanson, "The Way Things Linger," *Harvard Crimson*, December 10, 2018, https://www.thecrimson.com/article/2018/12/10/consequences/.

6. "Brown, Gylling Named Captains as Men's Soccer Announces Team Awards," Go Crimson (Harvard Athletics website), December 14, 2016, https://www.gocrimson.com/sports/msoc/2016-17/releases/20161214h8pz7p (page removed as of July 13, 2020).

7. Wait, you may ask, is it fair to paint Mr. Andrew Wheeler-Omiunu with this brush? It is. In their apology the soccer team says, "[We] fully grasp the gravity of our conduct, for which each member of our team takes full and equal responsibility." 2016 Harvard Men's Soccer Team, "An Apology from Harvard Men's Soccer."

8. Bethany McLean, "How Wells Fargo's Cutthroat Corporate Culture Allegedly Drove Bankers to Fraud," *Vanity Fair*, May 31, 2017, https://www.vanityfair.com/news/2017/05/wells-fargo-corporate-culture-fraud.

9. McLean, "Wells Fargo's Cutthroat Corporate Culture."

10. Bess Levin, "6 Ways Wells Fargo Made Its Employees' Lives a Living Hell," *Vanity Fair*, April 10, 2017, https://www.vanityfair.com/news/2017/04/wells-fargo-john-stumpf-carrie-tolstedt.

11. E. Scott Reckard, "Wells Fargo's Pressure-Cooker Sales Culture Comes at a Cost," *Los Angeles Times*, December 21, 2013, https://www.latimes.com/business/la-fi-wells-fargo-sale-pressure-20131222-story.html.

12. McLean, "Wells Fargo's Cutthroat Corporate Culture."

13. McLean, "Wells Fargo's Cutthroat Corporate Culture."

14. Reckard, "Wells Fargo's Pressure-Cooker Sales Culture Comes at a Cost."

15. Reckard, "Wells Fargo's Pressure-Cooker Sales Culture."

16. J. D. Morris, "Wells Fargo Scandal Foreshadowed in St. Helena Woman's Lawsuit," *Santa Rosa (CA) Press Democrat*, October 8, 2016, https://www.pressdemocrat.com/news/6161292-181/wells-fargo -scandal-foreshadowed-in.

17. Anonymous, "Whistleblower: Wells Fargo Fraud 'Could Have Been Stopped,'" CBS News, August 2018, https://www.cbsnews .com/news/whistleblower-wells-fargo-fraud-could-have-been -stopped/.

18. Stacy, Cowley "At Wells Fargo, Complaints About Fraudulent Accounts Since 2005," *New York Times*, October 11, 2016, sec. Business, https://www.nytimes.com/2016/10/12/business/dealbook/at-wells -fargo-complaints-about-fraudulent-accounts-since-2005.html.

19. "Unauthorized Wells Fargo Accounts," interview of Wells Fargo CEO John Stumpf by Senate Banking, Housing, and Urban Affairs Committee, C-SPAN, September 20, 2016, video, 3:51:27, https:// www.c-span.org/video/?415547-1/ceo-john-stumpf-testifies- unauthorized-wells-fargo-accounts&start=641.

20. Ann Marsh, "Unprotected: How the Feds Failed Two Wells Fargo Whistleblowers," *American Banker*, August 14, 2017, https://www .americanbanker.com/news/unprotected-how-the-feds-failed-two- wells-fargo-whistleblowers.

21. Kristin Broughton, "Do Problems with Lender-Placed Auto Insurance Go Beyond Wells?," *American Banker*, August 8, 2017, https:// www.americanbanker.com/news/do-problems-with-lender-placed -auto-insurance-go-beyond-wells.

22. I once sang his praises: Grant McCracken, "Charlie Rose vs. George Lucas. Culture by Commotion," *CultureBy—Grant McCracken* (blog), 2016, https://cultureby.com/2016/08/charlie-rose-vs-george-lucas.html.

23. Amy Brittain and Irin Carmon, "Charlie Rose's Misconduct Was Widespread at CBS and Three Managers Were Warned, Investigation Finds," *Washington Post*, May 3, 2018, https://www.washingtonpost.com/charlie-roses-misconduct-was-widespread-at-cbs-and-three-managers-were-warned-investigation-finds/2018/05/02/80613d24-3228-11e8-94fa-32d48460b955_story.html.

24. Rachel Abrams and John Koblin, "At '60 Minutes,' Independence Led to Trouble, Investigators Say," *New York Times*, December 6, 2018, https://www.nytimes.com/2018/12/06/business/media/60-minutes-jeff-fager-don-hewitt.html.

25. Barry Glendenning, "Whatever Your Opinion on Lance Armstrong, Liking His Podcast Is Not a Sin," *The Guardian*, July 22, 2017, https://www.theguardian.com/sport/2017/jul/22/lance-armstrong-podcast-tour-de-france-cycling.

26. William Edwards, "Lance Armstrong's Latest Feat: Returning to Public—and Corporate—Favor," CNBC, July 22, 2018, https://www.cnbc.com/2018/07/18/lance-armstrongs-return-to-public--and-corporate--favor.html.

27. This is not a quote from Lance Armstrong. It is invented for expositional purposes.

### CHAPTER 2: UNSUNG HEROES

1. Jean-Jacques Rousseau, *The Social Contract*, trans. Maurice Cranston (London: Penguin Classics, 1968).

2. Alexis de Tocqueville, *Democracy in America* (New York: Harper-Collins, 1966).

3. Carroll Doherty, "7 Things to Know About Polarization in America," Pew Research Center, June 12, 2014, http://www.pewresearch.org/fact-tank/2014/06/12/7-things-to-know-about-polarization-in-america/.

4. Grant McCracken, "Donald Trump Is a Fireship," *CultureBy—Grant McCracken* (blog), September 15, 2015, https://cultureby.com/2015/09/donald-trump-as-a-fireship.html.

5. I have added, omitted, and changed details of Jim's life to protect his anonymity.

6. Stacey Bewkes, "The Cheese Stands Alone," *Quintessence* (blog), December 13, 2010, https://quintessenceblog.com/the-cheese-stands-alone/.

7. Lee Jennings, testimonial, Taste Life Twice, accessed July 14, 2020, https://www.tltwriting.com/cheers-for-tlt.html.

8. Cathy Bonczek, testimonial, Taste Life Twice, accessed July 14, 2020, https://www.tltwriting.com/cheers-for-tlt.html.

## CHAPTER 3: HONOR, AN EARLY EXPERIMENT

1. "Elizabeth's Tilbury Speech: July 1588," British Library, accessed July 14, 2020, http://www.bl.uk/learning/timeline/item102878.html.

2. "Queen Elizabeth I (Cate Blanchett), Tilbury Speech," excerpt from *Elizabeth: The Golden Age* (2007), uploaded by user Kwokshee, May 7, 2011, video, 1:48, https://www.youtube.com/watch?v=T3Bq1h728X0&ab_channel=kwokshsee.

3. Arthur F. Kinney and Thomas Warren Hopper, eds., *A New Companion to Renaissance Drama* (Hoboken, NJ: Wiley-Blackwell, 2017), 82.

4. Ibid.

## CHAPTER 4: AMERICAN POSTCARDS

1. This account of the avant-garde impulse relies on my treatment of the topic in Grant McCracken, *Chief Culture Officer* (New York: Basic Books, 2009).

2. Paul Smith, *Seurat and the Avant-garde* (New Haven: Yale University Press, 1997); Renato Poggioli, *The Theory of the Avant-garde*, trans. Gerald Fitzgerald (Cambridge, MA: Harvard University Press, 1968), 114.

3. "Sad Young Man," *Time*, November 1, 1926, http://content.time.com/time/magazine/article/0,9171,1117075,00.html.

4. Kathleen Adler, Erica Hirshler, and H. Barbara Weinberg, *Americans in Paris 1860–1900* (London: National Gallery, 2006); Sophie Lévy, *A Transatlantic Avant-garde: American Artists in Paris, 1918–1939* (Berkeley: University of California Press, 2004).

5. Michael Reynolds, *Hemingway: The American Homecoming* (New York: W. W. Norton, 1992), 99.

6. The following account of the Beats is indebted to Steven Watson's *The Birth of the Beat Generation: Visionaries, Rebels, and Hipsters, 1944–1960* (New York: Pantheon Books, 1995).

7. Watson, *The Birth of the Beat Generation*, 3, 75–76; Herbert Huncke, *Guilty of Everything* (New York: Paragon House, 1990); Norman Mailer, *The White Negro: Superficial Reflections on the Hipster* (San Francisco: City Lights Books, 1957).

8. Nicholas Hewitt, "Shifting Cultural Centers in Twentieth-Century Paris," in *Parisian Fields*, ed. Michael Sheringham (London: Reaktion Books, 1996), 30–45.

9. Watson, *The Birth of the Beat Generation*, 15–16.

10. Watson, *The Birth of the Beat Generation*, 98, 127–28, 138.

11. "The only people for me are the mad ones, the ones who are mad to live, mad to talk, mad to be saved, desirous of everything at the same time, the ones who never yawn or say a commonplace thing, but burn, burn, burn, like fabulous yellow Roman candles explod-

ing like spiders across the stars, and in the middle, you see the blue center-light pop, and everybody goes ahh. . . ." Jack Kerouac, *On the Road* (New York: Viking Press, 1957), 5.

12. Wikipedia, s.v. "hippie," last modified July 4, 2020, http://en.wikipedia .org/wiki/Hippie.

13. This quote and previous are from "Youth: The Hippies," *Time*, July 7, 1967, http://content.time.com/time/magazine/article/0,9171,899555,00 .html.

14. Lionel Trilling, *Sincerity and Authenticity* (Cambridge, MA: Harvard University Press, 1972).

15. Meghan Markle, "Meghan Markle on Why 'Being Enough' Changed Everything," *Darling*, November 6, 2018, https://darlingmagazine.org /meghan-markle-career/.

16. Trilling spoke of "detaching the reader from the habits of thought and feeling that the larger culture imposes, of giving him a ground and a vantage point from which to judge and condemn, and perhaps revise, the culture that produced him." Lionel Trilling, *Beyond Culture: Essays on Literature and Learning* (New York: Penguin Books, 1965), 12.

17. A. Z. Yu et al., "Pantheon 1.0, a Manually Verified Dataset of Globally Famous Biographies, *Scientific Data* 3, 150075 (2016), doi: 10.1038 /sdata.2015.75.

18. Daniel J. Boorstin, *The Image: A Guide to Pseudo-Events in America* (New York: Harper and Row, 1961); Christopher Lasch, *The Culture of Narcissism: American Life in an Age of Diminishing Expectations* (New York: W. W. Norton, 1978).

19. "Woo Girls! How I Met Your Mother," excerpt from *How I Met Your Mother*, season 1, episode 1 (2005), uploaded by user Joe Jenkins, October 7, 2016, video, 2:00, https://www.youtube.com/watch ?v=V8yUhUXl-oY.

20. American Society of Plastic Surgeons, *2018 Plastic Surgery Statistics Report*, 2018, https://www.plasticsurgery.org/documents/News/Statistics/2018/plastic-surgery-statistics-full-report-2018.pdf; Catherine Saint Louis, "When That Smile Is Too Perfect," *New York Times*, October 19, 2010, https://www.nytimes.com/2010/10/21/fashion/21SKIN.html.

21. Tom Peters, "The Brand Called You," *Fast Company*, August/September 1997, http://www.fastcompany.com/magazine/10/brandyou.html.

22. Stuart Dredge, "Another YouTuber—Lilly Singh—Hits the Exhaustion Wall," Musically, November 14, 2018, https://musically.com/2018/11/14/another-youtuber-lilly-singh-hits-the-exhaustion-wall/.

23. Zach Braff, 2019, "In the Time It Takes to Get There," https://youtu.be/QWIblC4rEL0

24. Jon Caramanica, "This 'Imagine' Cover Is No Heaven," *New York Times*, March 20, 2020, https://www.nytimes.com/2020/03/20/arts/music/coronavirus-gal-gadot-imagine.html. Caramanica says, "Imagine" is "pummeled and stabbed, disaggregated, stripped for parts and left for trash collection by the side of the highway." Tavi Gevinson satirized the star-studded effort. Tavi Gevinson (@tavitulle), "You may have seen the viral video of celebrities singing the song Imagine," Instagram video, March 19, 2020, https://www.instagram.com/p/B97awVtlkWh/?utm_source=ig_web_copy_link.

25. Andrea Park, "Madonna Slammed for Self-Centered VMAs Tribute to Aretha Franklin," *CBS News*, August 21, 2018, https://www.cbsnews.com/news/madonna-slammed-for-self-centered-vmas-tribute-to-aretha-franklin/; Matthew Dessem, "Madonna's Eurovision Performance Somehow Fails to Solve Israeli-Palestinian Conflict," *Slate*, May 19, 2019, https://slate.com/culture/2019/05/eurovision-2019-madonna-tel-aviv-israel-like-a-prayer.html; Kay Hymowitz, "Ricky

Gervais Read America," *City Journal*, January 7, 2020, https://www.city -journal.org/ricky-gervais-golden-globes.

26. Kenneth T. Jackson, *Crabgrass Frontier: The Suburbanization of the United States* (New York: Oxford University Press, 1987).

27. Grant McCracken, *Transformations: Identity Construction in Contemporary Culture* (Indianapolis: Indiana University Press, 2008).

28. John Cheever, *Bullet Park* (New York: Knopf, 1969), 66.

29. Donald R. Katz, *Home Fires: An Intimate Portrait of One Middle-Class Family in Postwar America* (New York: Perennial, 1993).

30. I have drawn some of these details from an early treatment of the topic in Grant McCracken, *Culture and Consumption II: Markets, Meaning, and Brand Management* (Indianapolis: Indiana University Press, 2005), and Grant McCracken, *Transformations: Identity Construction in Contemporary Culture* (Indianapolis: Indiana University Press, 2008).

31. "Autos: Step to the Rear," *Time*, November 28, 1955, 82.

32. "Buick: Flight into Anywhere," advertisement, *Time*, July 16, 1956, 29; "Oldsmobile: 'Dream Car,'" advertisement, *Life*, February 22, 1954, 42–43; "Buick: Thrill of the Year Is Buick," advertisement, *Maclean's*, March 19, 1955, 37; "Studebaker: Craftsmanship with a Flair," advertisement, *Time*, November 28, 1955, 8; "Plymouth Hikes '56 Ad Budget 18%; Seeks to Garner 11½% of Market," *Advertising Age* 26, no. 41 (1955): 2, 114.

33. John G. Cawelti, *Apostles of the Self-Made Man: Changing Concepts of Success in America* (Chicago: University of Chicago Press, 1965), 12.

34. Saul Bellow, foreword to *The Closing of the American Mind*, by Allan Bloom (New York: Simon & Schuster, 1987), 13.

35. Daniel Bell, *The Cultural Contradictions of Capitalism* (New York: Basic Books, 1976).

36. Max Weber, *Economy and Society*, ed. Guenther Roth and Claus Wittich (Los Angeles: University of California Press, 1978), 2: 959.

37. Jane Ciabattari, "Hobbits and Hippies: Tolkien and the Counterculture," *BBC Culture*, November 19, 2014, https://www.bbc.com/culture/article/20141120-the-hobbits-and-the-hippies.

38. Gertrude Himmelfarb, *On Liberty and Liberalism: The Case of John Stuart Mill* (New York: Knopf, 1990).

39. Todd Gitlin, *The Sixties: Years of Hope, Days of Rage* (New York: Bantam, 1993).

40. Josh Karp, *A Futile and Stupid Gesture: How Doug Kenney and National Lampoon Changed Comedy Forever*, 1st ed., (Chicago: Chicago Review Press, 2006), 297.

41. Steve King, Anthony Townsend, and Carolyn Ocklels, *The New Artisan Economy*, Intuit Future of Small Business Series (Palo Alto, CA: Institute for the Future, 2008), http://http-download.intuit.com/http.intuit/CMO/intuit/futureofsmallbusiness/SR-1037C_intuit_future_sm_bus.pdf.

42. I simplify for the sake of brevity. A more complete account of the artisanal trend would have to look at the influence of Danny Meyer, Ruth Reichl, Thomas Keller, James Beard, Mark Miller, Wolfgang Puck, and David Bouley, among others.

43. David Kamp, *The United States of Arugula* (New York: Broadway, 2006), 133.

44. Josh Adler, "Alice Waters: Still Touting Simple Food," *Newsweek*, September 30, 2007, https://www.newsweek.com/alice-waters-still

-touting-simple-food-99817; Marian Burros, "What Alice Taught Them: Disciples of Chez Panisse," *New York Times*, September 26, 1984, sec. Home & Garden, https://www.nytimes.com/1984/09/26 /garden/what-alice-taught-them-disciples-of-chez-panisse.html.

45. Isis Aquarian, "Really well done and thank you," January 1, 2015, comment on FatherYod.jpg by copyright holder, Wikipedia, s.v. "Father Yod," https://en.wikipedia.org/w/index.php?title=File:Father_ Yod.jpg&oldid=665109446.

46. Ronda Kaysen, "Food Start-Ups Flock to Old Pfizer Factory in Brooklyn," *New York Times*, March 27, 2012, http://www.nytimes .com/2012/03/28/business/food-start-ups-flock-to-old-pfizer -factory-in-brooklyn.html; Benjamin Wallace, "The Twee Party: Is Artisanal Brooklyn a Step Forward for Food or a Sign of the Apocalypse?," *New York*, April 13, 2012, http://nymag.com/news/features /artisanal-brooklyn-2012-4/. If you ever get a chance, have a walk around the old Pfizer building on Flushing Avenue in Brooklyn. It's very large artisanal experiment.

47. Jason Kosmas and Dushan Zaric, *Speakeasy: The Employees Only Guide to Classic Cocktails Reimagined* (New York: Ten Speed Press, 2010); Camper English, "Has the Mixology Movement Created a Monster?," 7X7, February 22, 2011, http://www.7x7.com/eat-drink/has -mixology-movement-created-monster.

48. Adam Tschorn, "Normcore Is (or Is It?) a Fashion Trend (or Non-Trend or Anti-Trend)," *Los Angeles Times*, May 18, 2014, https:// www.latimes.com/style/la-ig-normcore-20140518-story.html.

49. Marcelle Sussman Fischler, "Suburban Buyers Ask: Can I Walk to Town?," *New York Times*, December 16, 2016, https://www.nytimes .com/2016/12/16/realestate/suburban-buyers-ask-can-i-walk-to-town .html.

NOTES

50. "A Conversation with Robert Greenblatt, Chairman, NBC Entertainment," October 27, 2016, Paley Center for Media, video, 45:27, https://www.paleycenter.org/mc-greenblatt-10-27.

51. Alex Williams, "A Negroni Summer," *New York Times*, August 20, 2014, sec. Fashion, https://www.nytimes.com/2014/08/21/fashion/a-negroni-summer.html; N. J. Falk, n.d., "Entertaining: The Apéritif Culture Is Making a Comeback," *Forbes*, accessed March 21, 2020, https://www.forbes.com/sites/njgoldston/2019/05/22/entertaining-new-start-up-haus-is-poised-to-lead-the-comeback-of-the-aperitif-culture/.

52. Ryan Irvine, "Let's Slow Things Down and Bring Back the Pre-Dinner Drink," *Cleveland Scene*, January 22, 2014, https://www.clevescene.com/cleveland/apandeacuteritifs-lets-slow-things-down-and-bring-back-the-pre-dinner-drink/Content?oid=3771218; N. J. Falk, n.d., "Entertaining: The Apéritif Culture Is Making a Comeback," *Forbes*, accessed May 22, 2019, https://www.forbes.com/sites/njgoldston/2019/05/22/entertaining-new-start-up-haus-is-poised-to-lead-the-comeback-of-the-aperitif-culture/.

53. David E. Shi, *The Simple Life: Plain Living and High Thinking in American Culture* (New York: Oxford University Press, 1985); Tibor Scitovsky, *The Joyless Economy: An Inquiry into Human Satisfaction and Consumer Dissatisfaction* (New York: Oxford University Press, 1976).

54. This is what the Griff shows, using, among other things, stats from Reddit: https://subredditstats.com/r/okboomer.

55. Chris Will, "Hook & Reel: Looking Back at Grimes' Cosmic 'Art Angels' Album," *B-Sides & Badlands*, November 6, 2017, https://bsidesbadlands.com/grimes-art-angels-anniversary-album-review/.

56. Brian Hiatt, "Grimes: Live from the Future," *Rolling Stone*, March 5, 2020, https://www.rollingstone.com/music/music-features/grimes-rolling-stone-digital-cover-960843/.

192

57. Keith Thomas, *Religion and the Decline of Magic* (London: Weidenfeld and Nicholson, 1971).

58. Henry Jenkins, *Convergence Culture: Where Old and New Media Collide* (New York: NYU Press, 2006).


## Chapter 5: Honor's Refuge

1. James Bowman, *Honor: A History* (New York: Encounter Books, 2006).

2. Adam Kirsch, "Does Honor Matter?," *The Atlantic*, June 3, 2018, https://www.theatlantic.com/entertainment/archive/2018/06/why-honor-matters-review/561788/.

3. Rich Lowry, *The Case for Nationalism: How It Made Us Powerful, United, and Free* (New York: Broadside Books, 2019), 105.

4. Tom Cotton, *Sacred Duty: A Soldier's Tour at Arlington National Cemetery* (New York: William Morrow, 2019), 1.

5. Cotton, 173.

6. Cotton, 171.

7. Sandra Gibson, "The Code of Honor; Know It, Embrace It," US Army, March 8, 2013, https://www.army.mil/article/98038/the_code_of_honor_know_it_embrace_it.


## Chapter 6: Rebuilding Honor

1. Marshall Sahlins, *Stone Age Economics* (Chicago: Aldine Transaction, 1972).

2. Sir Thomas Elyot, *The Boke Named the Governour* (1531; London: J. M. Dent and Co., 1907), 130.

3. Alan Dershowitz, interview by Ben Shapiro, *The Ben Shapiro Show Sunday Special*, March 8, 2020, podcast, MP3 audio, 1:05:11, https://www.listennotes.com/podcasts/the-ben-shapiro-show/alan-dershowitz-the-ben-cso6Ydez20i/.

4. Lionel Trilling, *Sincerity and Authenticity* (Cambridge, MA: Harvard University Press, 1972).

5. Trilling spoke of "detaching the reader from the habits of thought and feeling that the larger culture imposes, of giving him a ground and a vantage point from which to judge and condemn, and perhaps revise, the culture the produced him." Trilling, *Beyond Culture*, 12.

6. Brittain and Carmon, "Charlie Rose's Misconduct."

7. Jack Shafer, "Sean Spicer Is Washington's First Pariah," *Politico Magazine*, September 21, 2017, https://www.politico.com/magazine/story/2017/09/21/jack-shafer-sean-spicer-pariah-215634.

8. Megan Bronson, "The Dynamics of Shame and Addiction," Phoenix Society for Burn Survivors, August 27, 2019, https://www.phoenix-society.org/resources/breaking-free-of-the-addiction-shame-cycle.

9. Michael Wines, "Against Drug Tide, Only a Holding Action," *New York Times*, June 24, 1988, sec. New York, https://www.nytimes.com/1988/06/24/nyregion/against-drug-tide-only-a-holding-action.html.

10. Timothy Egan, "Crack's Legacy: A Special Report; A Drug Ran Its Course, Then Hid With Its Users," *New York Times*, September 19, 1999, sec. U.S., https://www.nytimes.com/1999/09/19/us/crack-s-legacy-a-special-report-a-drug-ran-its-course-then-hid-with-its-users.html.

11. Joe Houchins, "Can You Get Addicted to Crack After the First Use?," Drugabuse.com, last modified September 5, 2019, https://drugabuse.com/crack/first-time-use/.

# NOTES

12. Egan, "Crack's Legacy."

13. Egan, "Crack's Legacy."

14. This image is by Hans Holbein the Younger. It belongs to the British Royal Collection Trust. "Hans Holbein the Younger (1497/8–1543): Sir Thomas Elyot (c.1490–1546) c. 1532–4," Royal Collection Trust, accessed July 14, 2020, https://www.rct.uk/collection/912203/sir -thomas-elyot-c-1490-1546.

15. "Who We Are," Middle Collegiate Church of New York, accessed July 14, 2020, https://www.middlechurch.org/who-we-are.

16. Sir Thomas Elyot puts it this way: "[I]n every thyng is ordre, and without ordre may be nothing stable or permanent; and it may nat be called ordre, excepte it do contain in it degrees, high and base." Elyot, *The Boke Named the Governour*, 4.

17. William J. Bennett, *The Book of Virtues* (New York: Simon & Schuster, 2010).

# ABOUT THE AUTHOR

Grant McCracken is a cultural anthropologist. He holds a PhD from the University of Chicago. He is the author of twelve books, including most recently *Culturematic*, *Flock and Flow*, and *Dark Value*. He is the founder of the Institute of Contemporary Culture at the Royal Ontario Museum. Grant has taught briefly at Harvard, University of Cambridge, and MIT. He is a cofounder of the Artisanal Economies Project. He is the inventor of the Griff, an early warning system for social and cultural change. He consults widely, including for Google, the Ford Foundation, Kanye West, Netflix, Samuel Adams, the Boston Book Festival, Oprah, PBS, State Farm, NBC, IBM, Nike, and the White House.